GRIT
DON'T
QUIT

Also by

BIANCA JUÁREZ OLTHOFF

Play with Fire
How to Have Your Life Not Suck

GRIT DON'T QUIT

Developing Resilience and Faith When Giving Up Isn't an Option

Bianca Juárez Olthoff

W PUBLISHING GROUP

AN IMPRINT OF THOMAS NELSON

Published in Nashville, Tennessee, by W Publishing, an imprint of Thomas Nelson.

Author is represented by the literary agency of The Fedd Agency, Inc., P. O. Box 341973, Austin, Texas 78734.

Thomas Nelson titles may be purchased in bulk for educational, business, fundraising, or sales promotional use. For information, please email SpecialMarkets@ThomasNelson.com.

ISBN 978-1-4003-3623-4 (audiobook)
ISBN 978-1-4003-3622-7 (eBook)
ISBN 978-1-4003-3621-0 (TP)

Library of Congress Control Number: 2022950307

Printed in the United States of America
23 24 25 26 27 LBC 5 4 3 2 1

To the man who has picked me up after countless falls, kissed my bruised knees, and whispered "No blood, no pain." I am forever indebted to you.

Dad, I love you more than beans and rice and chips and salsa. No one has taught me more about resilience than you. Adapt, overcome, innovate, por vida!

CONTENTS

CONTENTS

SECTION THREE: THE POWER OF STAYING: IT WILL ALL BE WORTH IT

SIGN ON THE DOTTED LINE

Have you ever had one of those moments when you just wanted to give up? Facing the choice to throw in the towel or keep fighting, you'd rather just toss that towel and peace out?

You're spent.

You're exhausted.

Your chest is heavy.

Your heart is weary.

There's a part of you that wishes for a new day—heck, maybe even a new life—and you must somehow muster enough strength to show up when all you want to do is stay in bed. No judgment here; I've been there plenty of times.

Sigh.

But what if I told you that if you don't quit, you will find a way to make it through?

What if I told you that failing is acceptable, losing is acceptable, and crying is acceptable, but quitting is not?

Well, friend, that's *exactly* what I'm telling you. You can cry, but you can't quit.

If you're reading this book, it's most likely because you've found yourself feeling knocked down. Whether it's a job loss, life transition, or heartbreak, you're feeling tired, weary, and defeated. Can I affirm you? Can I give you a big high five? You might feel like giving up, but you've picked up this book—and that's a sign that you're already resilient!

I'm going to be bold and make you a promise. I promise that this book contains simple and specific instructions on becoming more resilient. My goal isn't simply to describe what it means to be resilient. Friends, that's been done before through a host of amazing books. What I'm committing to explore and explain in these chapters is *how* you can get there. Using story, science, and Scripture, I want to show you how to leverage your emotional pain or perceived failure and turn it into resilience. I will share tools that enable you to become resilient. I'm not simply going to list the traits of resilient people.

I believe without a doubt that there is, at the very least, a tiny ember of hope inside you. I want to stoke the fire and fan the flames. I want *you* to know that you can get back up and fight again, and I am going to show you how.

One survey in 2022 found that over 28 percent of respondents who started a book did not finish it.[1] So before you start this journey of developing grit, building resilience, and learning the power of perseverance, I'm boldly asking something of you: Will you promise to complete this book?

Yes, I'm serious. Why? Because we can't talk about perseverance and have you quit this book in the middle, now can we? Here is a promise we are making to each other. We are committing to the following:

I, <u>Bianca Juárez Olthoff</u>, solemnly swear to open my heart, share honestly, and provide helpful truths about how to become a resilient person, full of grit and perseverance. I am committed to seeing you step into your calling and live out your convictions, no matter the cost. I'm dedicated to speaking the truth and brimming with faith that it will allow you to step into true freedom.

Name: <u>Bianca Juárez Olthoff</u>
Signature:

Now it's your turn. Ready?

I, _____, solemnly swear to read this book and honestly evaluate places in my life where I'm stuck and spaces where I want to give up. I am committed to persevering and completing this book because I am resilient, and I want to get back up every time I'm down.

Name: _____
Signature: _____

No matter what season of life you're in, you aren't alone. I'm leaning in and whispering to you, "Get back up."

XO,
B

THE GOOD,
THE BAD,
AND THE UGLY

chapter one

GET BACK UP

The godly may trip seven times, but they will get up again.

PROVERBS 24:16 NLT

The crisp Saturday morning was draped in a cool haze, which hung heavy in the air as fans and families trickled into the large stadium. People carrying blankets and thermoses full of warm drinks found places to sit on the aluminum benches as the track-and-field officials and high school athletes stretched and prepared for a day of competition. Shivering, I found myself on the red-clay track between white chalk lines, legs shaking from nerves—I blamed the weather. My cleats crunched the ground as I made my way into my starting blocks. I pressed my feet tightly against the metal, held my hands steady, and coiled my body in anticipation, ready to spring out and start the race.

It was my junior year of high school, and I was voted captain of the varsity track team (a rarity for a nonsenior). The honor was not lost on me, and I was excited. All the training, conditioning, and sprints we ran for weeks on end had been to prepare us for *this* moment. Yes, *this* moment when students from all over the area would compete in a regional, preseason invitational, a way to show our stuff as well as gauge the threat of opponents for the season ahead.

I planned to compete in several events, but this race, the first of the day, was the 300-meter hurdles. Whatever possessed a MexiRican (that's *Mexican* plus *Puerto Rican*, in case you wondered) girl, five feet two on a tall day, to choose a sprint that required her to leap over ten aluminum obstacles, each three feet high, is beyond me. But I was raised by a faith-filled mother who would constantly quote scriptures like, "I can do everything through Christ, who gives me strength" (Philippians 4:13 NLT). Looking back, I'm not sure Paul the Apostle (the author of this famous verse) was specifically referring to teenage girls with the ambition of running track, but I appropriated the scripture as inspiration and confirmation that I was going to come out more than a conqueror! (Again, another nod to the wisdom of Paul the Apostle in Romans 8:37.)

Everyone was excited to start the full day of competition. There was electricity in the air; the anticipation felt as dense as the haze that clung to the ground. Before the girls in my race positioned into the staggered starting blocks, I was able to assess who I was up against—specifically, about whom I had been forewarned. These girls were in lanes on either side of me and stood as giants. In my memory, their hips were at my shoulders. Maybe I'm being dramatic, but in that moment, it felt like a David-versus-Goliath (and Goliath's sisters) battle.

Not to be discouraged by the size of my competitors, I attempted to hype myself up, whispering my favorite verse from Paul the Apostle: "Run in such a way as to get the prize" (1 Corinthians 9:24). Friend, if there is one thing I will run for, it's a prize. All eyes in the stadium were on this race, and I was running to win!

One of the track officials stood in the grass a short distance ahead of us and shouted, "On your marks!" We all settled into our blocks. "Get set!" he boomed, his right arm raised, pointing the starting pistol into the air. I could feel my muscles quiver, but I held my body still, waiting for the *pop* of the gun and the poof of white smoke signaling the start of the race.

Pow! The gun cracked, and I was out of the blocks like a jackrabbit. I could see Sister 1 on my outside lane, her long stride like a gazelle's as she sailed effortlessly over the first hurdle. I was only a few steps behind. As I approached the second hurdle, I hit a solid cadence—my pace actually matched hers! *I can't believe it,* I thought. *I can actually beat her!* We were coming up on the curve, and before I could process what was happening, Sister 2 was creeping up on my left. I could barely see her, but I could *feel* her—and she blew right past me at the third hurdle.

Now, this is the part of the story that haunts me to this very day, the decision that compromised what *might've* been had I just simply listened to what my coach had been telling me, day in and day out, the last two seasons. When training the hurdlers and sprinters, Coach Julia attempted to drill into our minds one cardinal rule of racing: "Don't look to your left or your right," she would tell us. "They're not your lanes. Your job is to run *your* race!" And during my third season, as captain of the varsity team, did I *at all* heed the wisdom of my beloved coach Julia? Nope, not even a little bit. My eyes darted back and forth between lanes, which completely threw off my approach to the next hurdle.

In the 300-meter hurdles, it's crucial to develop a rhythm between hurdles. If that cadence is interrupted, it will affect your body placement and your ability to get up and over the hurdle. Well, I let go of my focus long enough to break stride and cause my feet to stutter as I ran toward the fourth hurdle. I didn't have inertia working in my favor anymore, and I barely cleared it. The real problem with losing your rhythm and momentum in a hurdles race is that it's *very* hard to get it back.

This I discovered the hard way.

When I came up on the fifth hurdle, my knee, shin, and foot caught the top of the aluminum bar. I was thrown off balance and came down onto the clay with a *thud*. I looked up to see that Sister 1 and Sister 2 were long gone, but I believed I could still place third if I got back into it. I sprinted to the sixth hurdle, but the same problem occurred: I hadn't had time to build enough speed. I hadn't been able to get back in rhythm.

My foot caught the sixth hurdle and I scraped my knee. I fell again. Two competitors passed me.

I hit the seventh hurdle. I scraped my knee, scratched my shin, and fell with a *thud*. The rest of the runners flew past me.

My foot caught the eighth hurdle, and I fell hard on my hands and bloody knees. I was the only competitor left.

I tried to run my fastest on the final stretch of the track, but there was nothing more in me than a winded jog. As I approached the ninth hurdle, I was exhausted, and my increasingly labored breathing was now interrupted by my sobs. I felt pathetic and laughable, and this time, when I collided with the hurdle, it came down with me . . . into the dirt of the track in front of the crowded yet now-silent stadium.

I stood up with blood trickling from my knees, dripping onto my shins, and rolling toward my ankles. My hands were mottled with bits of red clay. Feebly, I limped toward the final hurdle and stood, depleted, in front of it. Then, with all the strength I had left, I literally picked up my left leg and flung it over the top. I was straddling the hurdle, eyes burning with tears and heart aching from embarrassment, but I picked up my right leg and hoisted it up and over too.

I heard a slow clap arise from a random observer, apparently trying to encourage me as I inched toward the end of the race. This, however, did not make me feel better.[i] All I wanted was for the earth to open up and swallow me whole. Once I finally managed to drag my aching body across the finish line, I collapsed on the track and cried hot, salty tears.

The next thing I knew, an ambulance drove onto the track. (Yes, they called an *ambulance*. In fairness, there *was* a lot of blood.) I was placed on a gurney and wheeled to the first-aid station. Coach Julia ran into the tent, where a nurse was tending to my scrapes and battle wounds. Julia flung her arms around me and said, "I'm so proud of you!" At this point I was sobbing and hardly able to form words of response. When my breathing slowed and I finally managed to get something out, I told her how I was sorry to have let her down, to have let the team down, and to have let *myself* down. "I completely failed, and I'm so embarrassed," I said, and fresh tears poured from my eyes again.

"Bianca, you should be proud of what happened on that track! No matter how hard it was, you showed us that you're not a quitter. You didn't stop! You. Got. Back. Up!"

---

i. To the lone clapper in the stands, thank you for your encouragement, but it didn't catch on. No one joined in, and it made the whole situation awkward.

Mindset

What makes people resilient? Are some of us simply born with grit—a courageous resolve not to give up?

I recently had a conversation with a friend who's going through a bitter divorce. In this season of her life—filled with disappointment, hardship, and starting over—she told me she just wasn't born with a resilient spirit, and she didn't have the will or strength that others had to persevere. In short, she believed resilience couldn't be cultivated or developed. "You're either resilient or you aren't," she said, and she confessed that some nights she just wanted to fall asleep and not wake up. The idea of fighting for health and hope, or redeeming her history didn't feel like a possibility, let alone a priority.

Maybe that's where you are today. You are too tired to try, too exhausted to feel hopeful about what lies ahead. Maybe you feel like a failure, so faith seems far away. You might've even convinced yourself that giving up is the easiest option and mediocrity is the highest bar you can set. Your inner critic is luring you to stay down, whispering, *Just put on your stretchy pants, eat a whole can of Pringles, and binge the newest Netflix reality series. You've worked so hard—on yourself, with relationships, and at work—and where has it gotten you?*

Left unchecked, the voices in your mind will also condemn you. Yes, those sinister, self-sabotaging voices will chide you into resenting your life and then make you feel guilty about how much you take for granted. Your inner voices whisper, *Why are you complaining? There are starving orphans in the world who would eat anything handed to them and you're sad about your life? I mean, in the grand scheme of global issues like economic instability and waging wars, your life is great, right?* So you make a gratitude list, choose joy, and thank God you aren't living in a ramshackle hut in a forsaken wasteland. You might have a great job, a loving family, or a scholarship, or maybe you're part of the blessed population that has more than two pairs of shoes, so why should you be disappointed, right? Wrong.

This isn't about what you have or don't have. This is about *you* having honest conversations with yourself—like I have many times—asking, *Is something wrong with me? Why can't I get it together?* Without conscious awareness, we find ourselves using words like *always, never,* and *forever.* Intentionally or unintentionally, these words can contribute to all-or-nothing, black-or-white thinking, which is harmful because it interprets situations in inaccurate extremes. These conversations might sound like, *I'm always behind, never prepared, and forever falling over hurdles others seem to fly over.* You may find yourself watching the social media feed of the woman who woke up at 4 a.m., took a Pilates class, ate a carb-free breakfast, and is now doing a live video promoting her collagen peptides protein powder that gives her glowing skin and shiny hair. Staring at her glass full of promise and potential, you find yourself saying, "Uh, I'll have what she's having!"

I don't think I'm the type of person who would self-identify as resilient or born with an extra measure of perseverance. But that conversation with my friend left me wondering, *Are some people born resilient, and others are not? Is perseverance a skill only for the less fortunate, out of necessity and not tenacity? What type of people are resilient, and is resilience a skill you can teach others?*

I'm convinced that you can acquire grit, develop resilience, and discover perseverance. As with any discipline or skill, the more you focus on and develop these attributes, the more you improve.

In her groundbreaking book *Mindset: The New Psychology of Success*, Dr. Carol Dweck, a psychology professor at Stanford University, draws on years of research to prove that resilience *can* be learned and developed. She simply and powerfully makes the distinction between the *fixed mindset*—the belief that you're stuck with what you're born with, that you have only a certain amount of intelligence and character—and the *growth mindset*, "the belief that your basic qualities are things you can cultivate through your efforts."[1]

> You can acquire grit, develop resilience, and discover perseverance.

According to Dweck, a fixed mindset means you think your personal characteristics are "carved in stone."[2] You're smart or you're not. You're talented or you're not. You believe you were born with traits and characteristics that are available in finite amounts.

We all know these people. We might even *be* these people. If you only attempt things you know you'll be good at, and you give up quickly when something gets hard, you might have a fixed mindset. Here's another clue your mindset might be fixed: you don't want to put in the effort or do the work needed for the challenge or the change.

Conversely, you have a growth mindset when you have "the passion for stretching yourself and sticking to it, even (or especially) when it's not going well."[3] Cultivating a growth mindset means you like challenges, enjoy effort, and learn from mistakes. In other words, a growth mindset is a resilient mindset.

My favorite benefit of cultivating a growth mindset is the belief and conviction that potential is unknown. But work is required.

There was a Spanish phrase I grew up hearing from my Mexican father. He would say, "*Hechalè con ganas!*" There isn't a direct translation, but the best way to translate this phrase is, "Audaciously work and believe with all your might!" We don't know how things will work out, so *hechalè con ganas, amigo!*

You may be thinking, *That's my problem! I have a fixed mindset!* Your fixed mindset may be telling you you're stuck with it, but fear not! "People may start with different temperaments and different aptitudes," Dweck writes, "but it is clear that experience, training, and personal effort take them the rest of the way. . . . Although people may differ in every which way—in their initial talents and aptitude, interests, or temperaments—everyone can change and grow through application and experience."[4] Endurance always beats out enthusiasm.

If you have a fixed mindset and experience something traumatic, you believe that you aren't equipped to overcome it. In your mind, a single failure means you *are* a failure. But here's the good news: people who are willing to adopt a growth mindset are the ones who are known for taking the lemons life has given them and making lemonade. Yes, it's taking setbacks and using them as fuel for success.

Because resilience, grit, and perseverance can *indeed* be attained, there is hope no matter your circumstances. *Hechalè con ganas!*

Failure Isn't Final

How are resilience and grit different for Christians? Science can provide insight into how our brains work, and data can pinpoint characteristics of successful people, but what bearing does our faith have on the power to bounce back? Though the words *grit* and *resilience* aren't in the Bible, we can see these ideas permeate stories of biblical characters who refused to give up and relied on God's strength to make it through.

Moses was placed in the Nile River as a child, killed someone, survived plagues, led a complaining group of grumblers for forty years, and still persevered to the promised land.

David fought with lions, bears, and giants; he committed adultery and murder; his son turned against him in an attempted coup; and he is still known as the greatest king in Israel's history.

Hannah waited an unstated number of years in prayer, believing God's promise that her barren womb would bear a child, until she bore the prophet Samuel, who would impact the world.

Jacob worked seven years for the hand of the woman he loved, only to find out he'd been tricked into marrying her sister. He then worked seven more years to marry the woman of his dreams, refusing to give up even after being manipulated and deceived by her father.

By taking an integrated look at science, stories, and Scripture, I want us to evaluate how the idea of resilience, for a follower of Jesus, provides an eternal perspective. The lens through which we see failure and falling, success and sanctification, should be rooted in the Word of God. As King Solomon said, "The godly may trip seven times, but they will get up again" (Proverbs 24:16 NLT). Falling isn't failure. And failure isn't final.

> **Falling isn't failure. And failure isn't final.**

One individual who personifies resilience in the Bible is Paul (who was formerly known as Saul). Paul was an apostle who arguably encountered traumatic suffering while displaying resilience and grit to keep moving forward.

If you're not familiar with Paul the Apostle, we are going to unpack his life more thoroughly over the course of this book, but here is a small snapshot into the life of a man full of grit and resilience.

After cruelly oppressing followers of Jesus, Paul (still Saul at that time) had a radical encounter with God on the road to Damascus. God called him out and gave him specific directions on what to do next. When it came time for him to start a ministry and spread the gospel, Paul was met with skepticism, judgment, and fear from believers who didn't think he was an *actual* Christian because of his past persecution of believers (Acts 9:26). And that's just the tip of the iceberg! As he pressed toward his calling, Paul was also mocked, beaten, imprisoned, starved, shipwrecked, bitten by a snake, stranded, and abandoned by partners in ministry.

Yet through all his trauma, trials, and tribulation, Paul refused to give up. While imprisoned (a result of being accused by Jewish leaders of false teaching and defiling the temple), he wrote letters to churches throughout Europe declaring resilience in the face of his incarceration: "Now all glory to God, who is able, through his mighty power at work within us, to accomplish infinitely more than we might ask or think" (Ephesians 3:20 NLT). Yes, life knocked him down, but he refused to stay down. There were moments his life was a living hell, but he continued to persevere, living out the famous saying, "If you're going through hell, keep going."

How did he do it? How did Paul maintain resilience even when faced with unfathomable opposition? What principles can we learn from Paul to provide us with practical tools that can help us persevere?

Resilience isn't exclusive to the privileged or to the poor. It doesn't matter the color of your skin, the college you went to, or whether you went to college at all. It doesn't matter if you've lost a loved one, lost a job, or even lost your vision. Regardless of whether you work in the White House or a warehouse, the principles we uncover together will improve your ability to cope when you fall over life's hurdles. They can help *anyone* become emotionally stronger simply by not giving up.

And I want to be clear: living a life of grit isn't about success. In its simplest and rawest form, resilience is the ability to show up, endure pain, press on, and keep going—even if you're not winning. This applies to personal failures, unemployment, addiction, relationships, dieting, and every other struggle that is part of the human experience.

Success is not the same thing as resilience. Don't get me wrong: achieving greater levels of resilience is its own kind of success, but not necessarily success as the world defines it.

Get back up, friend.

Resilience isn't measured by outcome, achievements, or the number of problems you overcome. When you're successfully resilient, your problems may still exist—but you're forging ahead in the middle of the mess. We must remain relentless despite the world's constant message that failure is final.

My goal as you complete this book is to figuratively look you in the eye the way Coach Julia looked at me, full of fierce pride, saying, "I'm so proud of you! You didn't stop. You. Got. Back. Up."

Get back up, friend. Like my dad always says, *"Hechalè con ganas!"*

THE NITTY-GRITTY

Principles

- You can acquire grit, develop resilience, and discover perseverance.
- Falling isn't failure. And failure isn't final.
- Success is not the same thing as resilience.
- We must remain relentless despite the world's constant message that failure is final.
- Get back up, friend.

Paul's Wisdom

"I can do everything through Christ, who gives me strength." (Philippians 4:13 NLT)

Prayer

God, I'm at the end of myself, and I feel tired. My heart wants to keep fighting, but my head says to quit. With all my strength, I am crying out to You to fill me with Your power and perspective to keep going. This is all too much for me, but with Your strength, I know I can press forward. Help me grow my mindset and believe that a limitless God has limitless strength for me. In Jesus' name, amen.

chapter two

YOU'RE NOT QUITTING TODAY

*Now get up and go into the city, and you
will be told what you must do.*

JESUS TO SAUL, DAMASCUS ROAD (ACTS 9:6 NLT)

I woke up early and set my work clothes on the bed, neatly pressed, organized, and totally professional. I had prepared for my largest work presentation to date. I had recently gotten married, and it felt like my entire life had been upended. Overnight and upon saying "I do," my "single" status was replaced with "spouse," "stepmom," and "pastor's wife." And as if that didn't feel like enough changes, I also accepted a brand-new job working at a global anti–human trafficking organization, A21.

While fighting the ills of modern-day slavery, I instantly inherited a five-year-old stepdaughter, Ryen, and seven-year-old stepson, Parker. Mornings in our house were a circus, comprised of making breakfast, packing lunches, bargaining over clothing choices, and combing hair. I knew the morning would be chaotic while trying to get the kids ready for school, so I made sure I was fully prepared early for my big meeting about rebranding a global nonprofit organization in nine countries.

I had worked on this project for three months, and our entire team was ready for the big pitch to our CEO and global manager. While my husband, Matt, cleaned up after breakfast, I changed into my perfectly ironed work clothes and called Ryen into the bathroom to comb her hair. Ryen had beautifully thick, wavy dark hair that sometimes got matted while she slept at night. That morning, she tugged and pulled at her hair, and I noticed her scratching behind her ears. I grabbed the detangling spray and comb, ready to put her hair into matching pigtails.

I sprayed her hair generously and grabbed a hair pick to make a perfect line down the center of her head. I pulled her locks apart like two heavy curtains and noticed little black-and-white dots all over her hair and scalp. I assumed the detangler mist hadn't sunk in properly, so I dragged the comb through her mane again. But the dots didn't disappear. In fact, the dots *moved*.

I leaned down toward Ryen's tiny head and realized the dots were not drops of detangler mist. The dots were lice. Not just a few little creepy-crawlers but an entire infestation of parasitic insects making their home on my daughter's head.[i] I don't do bugs. Nope,

---

i. Yes, they are my stepchildren, but I don't refer to them as such. I refer to them as my son and daughter. I recognize I haven't birthed them, but I raised them as if I did. Ergo, I shall refer to them as mine. Carry on, dear reader.

no sir. Anything with more than two legs that crawls is from Satan, and I rebuke all insects in Jesus' mighty name! Amen.

I dropped the comb while I raised my arms and screamed in surrender. Matt came running down the hallway, panicked. "What happened?" he asked, worried. I tried to remain calm while Ryen looked at me, terrified, her eyes wide as saucers. I spoke emphatically, through gritted teeth, "Ryen has lice."

Sweet Ryen had no clue what lice were, but she knew they couldn't be good, likely based on how firmly I pressed my back against the bathroom wall, too afraid to come near her. Matt gently bent Ryen's head down and confirmed the infestation. She started crying. I started crying. Poor Matt was stuck between a wailing child who was confused and a wailing wife who was scared.

Explaining the importance of my meeting and all the work that had gone into preparation, I told Matt I had to leave early to set up for the presentation. He generously said he would handle things at home and go to the drugstore to get a lice treatment. Then I realized, as I was about to leave the bathroom, with all the drama that was called for in a situation like this: Ryen and I had been sharing a hairbrush all week.

I froze in panic and felt an insatiable urge to start scratching my head. Immediately, I flung my hands onto my head and started dragging my nails along my scalp so hard I was surprised a hole didn't form. I shrieked, "I think I have lice!" Matt tried calming me down, but it was a lost cause. I was convinced my whole scalp was a breeding ground and I was probably going to have to shave my head. Matt seated me on the edge of the bathtub and gently lowered my head as he began to look for bugs or larvae. He swore to me that he didn't see anything, but I made him search again. And again. And again. I just *knew* that I was a walking plague.

My eyes caught the time on my phone, and I saw that morning's proposal flash through my mind: the graphs we color-coded, the research we compiled, the changes we proposed, and the budget it would require. Three months of blood (from paper cuts), sweat (from a broken air conditioner), and tears (trying to get people to care about modern-day slavery) were on the line. But I only wanted to shave my head and go back to bed. "I can't do this! It's too much. I'm going to fail," I wailed. "I just want to quit."

Matt continued to scour my head for lice and insisted he didn't see anything, but just to be safe, I asked him to buy treatment for Ryen and me both. I sat on the bathtub and Ryen sat on the toilet, both of us crying and confused. Matt ran to the drugstore down the street and came back with three bottles of lice treatment (one for Ryen, one for me, and an extra one just in case). Like a drill sergeant, he ordered us to bend over the bathtub, flinging our hair over our heads, and he began scrubbing. And as he did, my neatly pressed shirt began to wrinkle, the pristine collar now soaking wet.

After my treatment, I wrapped a towel around my head and, still crying, walked into my bedroom. Rummaging through my closet for a new shirt, I yelled to no one in particular, "I just want to quit!" And then there was Matt, who after washing my hair with lice treatment had inspected for signs of the critters three more times. (Do you blame me for insisting?) He pulled me into his chest, wrapped his arms around me (not so much as a comforting gesture but in a you-need-to-calm-down-and-be-an-adult kind of way), and said, "You're not quitting today. Go to work, and I'll sort the kids. You've got this!" I didn't want to admit that he was right.

I pulled my hair back in a tight ponytail and put on a hat (just in case I *did* have lice). I didn't stop crying my whole drive to the office, but when I arrived, I wiped my tears, applied some lipstick, and walked through the doors in my newly changed but unironed shirt.

A lice infestation may not sound super traumatic or relatable to you, but there will be moments in life that feel like unexpected obstacles. As a new instant-mom with a new job and a huge presentation to pitch, the weight of an unexpected trial caused me—the same girl who limped over that high school finish line covered in her own blood—to want to quit.

You may not be a parent. You may not have a presentation to make. You may not have lice. (With all my heart, I hope you don't have lice!) But you *will* have moments when you feel like you want to quit.

Here's the thing: You already know what quitting feels like. See what happens when you don't.

Perseverance and Endurance

What causes people to get back up when they fall? What are the tools we need in order to bounce back after we've been knocked down? There are a few characteristics that are hallmarks of wildly successful people.[ii]

But there is one specific characteristic that can help us succeed

---

ii. I'm defining *success* holistically. The world's understanding of success revolves around money, media, and mansions. The success I'm talking about encompasses our God-desires like purpose, wholeness, health, and holiness.

in completing what we are called to. What is this characteristic? Grit.

The Bible's terms for grit are *perseverance* and *endurance*. It's been said that perseverance is "continued effort to do or achieve something despite difficulties, failure, or opposition."[1] Endurance is most often explained as the determination to keep working toward our desired goals regardless of external challenges and internal weariness. But if the specific word *grit* isn't mentioned in the Bible, why is it important to our faith?

In 2013, Dr. Angela Lee Duckworth, a psychology professor at the University of Pennsylvania, gave a TED Talk briefly describing her many years of research. Her presentation, "Grit: The Power of Passion and Perseverance," has received more than twenty-eight million views at the time of this writing. After years of research across all ethnic, socioeconomic, educational, and psychological demographics, Duckworth reported that "one characteristic emerged as a consistent predictor of success. And it wasn't good looks, physical health, and it wasn't IQ. It was grit."[2]

Duckworth said, "Grit is having stamina. Grit is sticking with your future, day in, day out, not just for the week, not just for the month, but for years, and working really hard to make that future a reality. Grit is living life like it's a marathon, not a sprint."[3]

Duckworth's research is unparalleled. The proof behind her scholarship is extensive. But when asked where grit comes from, the clear answer remains elusive to her—she doesn't know. Though it may be a mystery to Duckworth, I believe looking at the life of Paul the Apostle might give us some clues on how grit, perseverance, and endurance are forged. In short, how can we cultivate this spirit? How can we bounce back from a setback?

Conversation, Conversion, Calling

Saul's life was dramatically altered through a singular conversation with Jesus. That conversation led to a spiritual conversion, which ultimately gave way to the call of God for his life.

When Saul (later known as Paul) is introduced to us in Scripture, it's at a moment of insane growth for the early church. But Saul was not a follower of Jesus at all. In fact, he wanted to shut down the message of Jesus by any means necessary. We get a glimpse of this in the beginning chapters of the book of Acts. The church was exploding, and the gospel was spreading in Jerusalem and the surrounding region. As a church planter myself, I can attest to this simple truth: where there is multiplication, there is division. The church was growing exponentially while simultaneously being divided. There were also internal issues threatening unity and growth, ranging from persecution externally to prejudice internally between believers from different backgrounds. They needed leaders to help expand the church, and the prerequisite was that they be full of faith and the Holy Spirit.

There was much to be concerned about during this time of growth, but it also gives us a clue into the early life and times of Saul. He was on a warpath to stop the followers of Jesus from spreading the gospel—at any cost. Acts 8:1 says that Saul not only participated in the persecution of Christians but also witnessed the murder of Stephen, one of the early church leaders. Saul wanted to stop the followers of Jesus from spreading the good news and gaining more influence.

There will always be resistance against the things that will bring God glory! If your business, marriage, or dreams will bring God glory, then the Enemy will do everything he can to stop you. But just as the early church grew amid persecution, may you likewise press forward and multiply.

After the murder of Stephen, Saul was walking with his cronies to find more Christians. We are told in Acts 9:1 that he went to the high priest for help in locating the Christians in Damascus so he could take them as prisoners back to Jerusalem. But on his way, Saul, the confronter, was about to be confronted.

Check out the account in Acts 9:3–5:

As he neared Damascus on his journey, suddenly a light from heaven flashed around him. He fell to the ground and heard a voice say to him, "Saul, Saul, why do you persecute me?"

"Who are you, Lord?" Saul asked.

"I am Jesus, whom you are persecuting," he replied.

Saul had a conversation with the resurrected Christ that changed his life. Saul's Hebrew name means *desired*, but his Roman name, Paul, means *little*.[4] The man who had been feared, with public power and religious authority, was now calling himself "little." This was a humbling hiccup in his life plan. This wasn't on the agenda. I would argue that this was a hurdle that literally took Saul to the ground. But this conversation wasn't for condemnation; it was intended for conversion. The conversation revealed who Saul was fighting against (Jesus Himself) and what to do next (go into the city and await further instructions).

A *conversion* is a change in character. The Bible is full of stories about people who encountered God and had their lives radically changed.

David was a shepherd boy who went from a protector of his flock to a giant-slayer.

Peter went from a fisherman to a powerful fisher of men and preaching the gospel to thousands.

Mary Magdalene went from possibly being a prostitute to being a powerful proselyte.

And the list goes on. When we have an encounter with God—when we have a *conversation* with God—we cannot help but be changed.

When we find ourselves falling over life's hurdles, it's easy to want to stay down. We might even get angry with God because we're convinced our way is the best way. But if we decide to adhere to what God whispers to us after we've been knocked down, I believe it will help us remember our calling.

> When we have an encounter with God—when we have a *conversation* with God—we cannot help but be changed.

In Acts 9:4, we are told that Saul fell to the ground when the Lord confronted him on the road to Damascus, but he didn't stay there. And neither should we. Check out the beginning of verse 6: "Now get up . . ." Jesus told Saul to *get up*. We aren't supposed to live on the ground, cowering in condemnation or fear of failure. Yes, we *will* fall down. But we aren't created to live lying down. We need to get back up and prove to the world and ourselves that if we aren't dead, God's not done!

After Saul was told to *get up*, he was further instructed to *go*. The Lord told him to "go into the city" (v. 6). Getting back up isn't the final goal; it's only step one. After a conversation with God, you don't hang back and form a holy huddle; the goal is to go out to your surrounding area and do what God has created and called you to do.

I don't know what God is personally calling you to, but just as the voice from heaven stopped Saul in his dusty Damascus tracks, I pray that God stops you even now in this moment to tell you what you need to do. Do I hope you get a voice from heaven or some other divine epiphany? Yes, that would be awesome! But for most of us, it's going to be way less spectacular or supernatural. For some, it's going to mean reapplying for that job. For others, it's going to require forgiving a spouse. For some, it's going to mean serving in your local church even though you feel unqualified. Still others will be called to start a business after having declared bankruptcy.

It sounds crazy, right? Because it is. Standing back up and moving forward is so much harder than quitting and remaining down. Perhaps you're wondering, *Bianca, are you telling me God will ask me to do things that I think I'm not able to do?* Yes, that's exactly what I'm telling you. The more you trust God and His promises, the easier it gets. The more we obey God's Word and His promptings, the more we will see the fruit of obedience in our lives.

Trust me: small acts of obedience have large impact. Forgiving the person who offended you is not only biblical, it is beautiful. Not lying or gossiping about the person who hurt you is not only spiritual, it is supernatural. It might take a lot of discipline and faith up front, but God will bring clarity that what you are doing is right. Saul didn't know what was happening on the Damascus Road, but he would soon realize that what God wanted him to do would not be done in his strength but in the strength given to him by the Spirit of God. Years after his fall-down/get-up moment on the Damascus Road, Paul told the Romans that the same Spirit that raised Jesus Christ from the dead lived in them (Romans 8:11). Even better news, it lives in us too. It's the Holy Spirit living in us who will empower us to do the things that seem absolutely impossible.

At the end of Acts 9:6, Jesus gave Saul a third directive: *be prepared for further instruction*. The Lord said, "you will be told what you must do." If you're tracking with this celestial conversation, Saul was told to:

1. Get up.
2. Go.
3. Be prepared for further instruction.

Now, this all sounds lovely *in theory*. But think about how crazy it is. Saul was being asked to blindly trust God (because in Acts 9:8 we are told he was *literally* blind after encountering God on the Damascus Road). I don't know about you, but when I find myself knocked down and needing to get up and forge forward, I want a plan, I want steps, and I want directions! But obeying God, even when we can't see what lies ahead, is the most powerful thing we can do.

> **Obeying God, even when we can't see what lies ahead, is the most powerful thing we can do.**

When Saul decided to get back up off the Damascus Road, it's unlikely he ever thought his letters would be read by billions of people over thousands of years.

As he stumbled and moved forward into the city, I doubt he knew the effect he would have on the global church. Being blind himself, Saul probably never imagined that he would heal others. Saul, while waiting for his sight to return, could never have guessed the number of people he would disciple. Saul didn't know he would be in front of the most powerful people of his era and hold audience with kings. But note this: Saul's conversation with Jesus led to a spiritual conversion that led to the call upon his life that has affected *all* of Christianity as we know it today.

Why? He got back up.

This Is the Why

If we are faithful to move, God is faithful to lead. It's been said that a moving car is easier to guide than a parked one. We might not know what God is up to, but when we obey Him and are willing to move, He will guide us to where we need to be.

> **If we are faithful to move, God is faithful to lead.**

The day of the global rebrand pitch and Olthoff lice infestation, I wanted nothing more than to quit. It wasn't just because my daughter had lice. It was because of *all the things*, friends! I wanted desperately to be a good wife and good mom and good employee. I wanted to make a difference and change the world and help those in need. But it was *hard*! After six months of marriage, parenting, fighting human trafficking, and perceived constant failing, I just wanted to sit down, throw a pity party, and quit.

It's moments like this—when you're facedown on the Damascus

Road or on all fours after falling over the final hurdle—where you have to focus on the bigger picture. Don't miss this. You have to remember what God has called you to:

God gave you the job.
God opened the door for your degree.
God asked you to reconcile.
God entrusted you with your child.
God gave you the marriage.
God allowed you to start the business.

So you must fight for it.

Perhaps you feel knocked down and don't have the gumption to get back up. I'm going to ask you two simple questions: Do you know *what* God has called you to? Do you know *why* He has called you to do it? When you're able to articulate what you want and why you want it, you will tap into the resilience, grit, and perseverance needed to dust off and go where God tells you to go.

Will everything end up perfect? Will every problem be solved and wrapped in a bow? Absolutely not. I speak from experience because the day of the global rebrand pitch, I was late to the office and felt frazzled and unprepared for our meeting. The pitch was an absolute disaster. So bad, in fact, it was completely rejected—everything from vision to budget to implementation and, yes, the color scheme and font choices too.

On my drive home, I prayed desperately to God. I asked Him if I could quit. Not just quit my job but quit everything I felt responsible for. I was tired. I had put in so much energy and effort, and I felt like I had nothing to show for any of it that even came close to the outcomes I badly wanted.

The day after that failed pitch, I woke up and remembered what I was called to. *I'm called to freedom and fighting for those who can't fight for themselves.* After confirming that neither Ryen nor I had visible lice, I started my morning routine of making breakfast, packing lunches, bargaining over clothing choices, and combing hair with a new, clean comb.

Later that day, I met with my team to start over on our rebrand. In six short months, not only was the rebrand approved, the vision clarified, new initiatives set, and the website redone, but the increased effectiveness that came out of it all enabled us to reach even more people through rescue, advocacy, and awareness.

Years later, I realize the successful rebrand wasn't the win. The real victory was my commitment to our organization and my refusal to quit. That resilience grew out of my conviction—knowing what I was called to: to fight for justice and for freedom.

Bouncing back after falling down reinforced my sense of commitment not only to the organization where I was working but also to the call on my life. There would be many more times at A21 when I would feel like I had failed and would again contemplate quitting due to feelings of inadequacy. But the mission to end slavery kept me focused, and my daily engagement toward that end prepared me for one of my favorite memories from my season of serving A21.

For years, my role as chief storyteller at A21 was purely domestic, based out of the headquarters in California. I didn't speak with survivors, I didn't meet with survivors, and I didn't interact with survivors directly in any form. But all that changed when what was supposed to be an administrative and organizational training trip in Thessaloniki, Greece, turned into a rescue operation. The day before I was scheduled to leave, I received a phone call from my coworker in Greece. She asked me whether I spoke Spanish, and I answered honestly: "Well, it's basic, but I can order food and have a light conversation."

"Amazing!" she chirped almost immediately. "We need you to interpret and help get a girl out of a local jail who has been trafficked into the country."

What I said: "Oh, absolutely."

What I thought: *Are you kidding me?! My Spanish skills top out just past "Mas guacamole, por favor," and they want me to explain the punitive ramifications of illegal entry into the European Union while investigating possible human sex trafficking? This is a terrible idea!*

En route to Greece, I pulled out my journal and began writing down every possible Spanish phrase I knew that could prepare me for heading into jail upon landing. I began to pray: *I'm so ill-equipped for this. I have no idea what I'm doing. Lord, please help me.* I didn't hear an audible voice, but peaceful calm came over my mind. I felt God reminding me of all the research, failure, and fatigue that had caused me to want to give up when my presentation bombed. *All of that prepared me for this.* The dogged determination and unwillingness to give up reminded me of what I wanted and felt called to do: *I'm called to freedom and to fight for those who can't fight for themselves.*

We were able to rescue the young woman, even with my botched and basic Spanish interpretation. She was not only released from jail but was also reunited with her family. On the day of her departure from the shelter, I remember wrapping my arms around her and saying, "*Tú eres mi razón*"—which means, "You are my reason." Because that is exactly what she was: she was my reason; she was my *why*.

You may feel blind to where God is leading you. Don't freak out! It's normal. I've been there. But let's act like Saul and get up and go into the city, and God will show us what to do next.

THE NITTY-GRITTY

Principles

- You already know what quitting feels like. See what happens when you don't.
- The Bible's terms for grit are *perseverance* and *endurance*.
- When we have an encounter with God—when we have a *conversation* with God—we cannot help but be changed.
- Obeying God, even when we can't see what lies ahead, is the most powerful thing we can do.
- If we are faithful to move, God is faithful to lead.

Paul's Wisdom

"Who are you, Lord?" (Acts 9:5)

Prayer

Jesus, I want to know who You are. I want to know You. I want to have a conversation with You that changes me and reveals my true identity. Show me what it is You want me to do and where it is You want me to go. I believe Your calling for my life is bigger than I can see now, so give me faith for my future. No matter what knocks me down, give me Your strength to get back up. In Jesus' name, amen.

chapter three

PIZZA, PERSPECTIVE, PURPOSE, AND PIVOTING

I want to know Christ—yes, to know the power of his
resurrection and participation in his sufferings.

PAUL THE APOSTLE (PHILIPPIANS 3:10)

Growing up in our house, pizza was a treat that felt like a lux-ury. If there was pizza on the table, you knew it was Friday, because Friday was *payday*! We had an affectionate phrase in our home for the one day of the week that was reserved for family: Friday Family Fun Day! But before you envision handcrafted, arti-san dough and fresh-pulled mozzarella with vine-ripened tomatoes, please know it wasn't that. It was always—*always*—Little Caesars pizza. At that time, the inexpensive chain restaurant offered two medium pizzas at a buy-one-get-one-free rate that landed squarely within our family's budget. So for just ten dollars, we could celebrate our family traditions over gooey cheese and crisp, golden dough. And it was *delicious*.

As was the tradition, my mom allowed my twin sister, Jasmine, and me to ride our bikes four blocks to pick up the pizzas and bring them back in time for dinner. This would be a simple task if we lived in suburbia. But we lived in hoodurbia. As in, we lived in the *hood*. And if we ever forgot that little detail, the spray-painted gang signs everywhere you looked reminded everyone in the neighborhood who ran the streets.

One Friday, like any other, my sister and I hopped on our bikes to race down to Little Caesars. Jasmine and I felt very brave, cycling alone to fetch our family dinner, telling stories and talking trash the entire way there. We couldn't wait to gather around the table for our weekly tradition and dive into our favorite meal.

When we arrived at Little Caesars, Jasmine—the eldest[i] and bossiest kid in our family—pulled a crumpled ten-dollar bill from her shorts pocket and handed it to the unenthusiastic employee behind the counter. He passed us a long cardboard tray that held side-by-side pizzas, wrapped in paper, replete with smudged tomato sauce and oil stains. It was glorious! If we had been the children of Israel, Little Caesars pizza was our version of manna in the desert.

I volunteered to balance the pizza on my handlebars, but bossy Jasmine said she should do it. We were not even a few steps from the store when we were approached by some teenagers on their own

---

i. She's the eldest by *one* minute. Literally, one.

bikes. They were each probably thirteen years old (which seemed *way* older in my nine-year-old mind) and they formed a half circle around us. They weren't the vicious street gang members who spray-painted walls and marked their territory, but in my mind, they must've been their interns. With a tough face and hungry eyes, the leader of the crew rose on her bike pedals and shouted, "Give us your pizza!"

I looked at Jasmine and panicked. Not only was this our family dinner but this was also our *manna*! This was our once-a-week treat of deliciousness, and now we were at risk of losing it to pimple-faced pseudo-gangbangers? Terrified and frozen, I didn't say anything, but I did manage to shake my head side to side and indicate *No*. Another kid chirped from the back of the group in a cracking, pubescent voice, "Yeah, give us your pizza!"

This time Jasmine spoke. She clutched the long pizza box and issued a deep, defiant, "No." Her confidence gave me courage, so I said, "Let's get out of here," in a way that I hoped expressed my lack of amusement with these would-be pizza pilferers. Internally I was shaking; externally I refused to give up what was ours.

In a quick exchange of glances, Jasmine and I instinctively knew what to do. (That unspoken twin language is a *real* thing!) I placed both my feet on the pedals of my bike and sped toward the group of kids to form a barricade so Jasmine could cycle past on the outside. We pedaled so furiously we couldn't even talk. Once we reached our front porch, we jumped off our bikes and ran inside, pizza safely in hand.

Over piping-hot slices, Jasmine and I told the story of our heroics while our parents humored us, affirming our bravery.[ii]

---

ii. Our father was a United States Marine Corps corporal, and by his proud look, you'd think we'd just fought in Vietnam. He was beaming.

> **If you never envision the end, you'll give up in the middle.**

Jasmine and I knew how Fridays were supposed to go. We knew what the pizza meant to our family. We knew we weren't going to give out, give up, or give in. We stuffed our faces, and my heart burst with pride.

Even when threatened and paralyzed with fear, I never lost sight of what it would cost me to give up. In the same way, keep your eyes on the prize, friends. If you never envision the end, you'll give up in the middle.

Knocked Down, but Not Out

Just in case you're wondering whether you are resilient, let me put on a pleated skirt and grab my pom-poms, because I'm your cheerleader! You. Are. Doing. It. You are refusing to let life knock you out. Don't get me wrong: life may have knocked you down, but I'm reminding you that you haven't been knocked *out*.

Don't believe me?

- If you got out of bed and showered today, you are resilient!
- If you have decided to show up to work and do your job (even if you loathe where you work and your coworkers drain you), you have grit!
- If you have made even the smallest decision to invest in your spiritual, mental, emotional, or physical health, you are persevering!

- And if you are currently unshowered, lying in bed, unemployed, and eating more than you know you should, listen—you are *still* resilient because you've made a decision to read this book.

Give yourself a break and celebrate the small, daily wins. You're doing it! You are putting in effort and doing the work to become who, deep down inside, you know you are called to be.

Three Ps of Resilience

Now that the cheering is over, let's talk about a game plan. What's needed to be resilient? Is there a recipe for resiliency?

I promised you stories, science, and Scripture, so buckle up and get ready for some research to break down the understanding of resilience. There are scientific studies about resilience based on groups ranging from Holocaust survivors to urban youth, from bankrupt business owners to those who become billionaires. Researcher Diane Coutu from the *Harvard Business Review* compiled layers of research and discovered an overlap in the attributes of resilient people in three major areas—"A staunch acceptance of reality; a deep belief, often buttressed by strongly held values, that life is meaningful; and an uncanny ability to improvise."[1]

I'll save you the hours of reading and research by giving you an abbreviated version here. Coutu discovered resilient people possess similar characteristics no matter their gender, ethnicity, or social standing. Her academic terminology is fabulous but rather complex. To make things simple, I've synthesized her research and put it into terms we can unpack together.

Three Ps of Resilience

Perspective—an honest acceptance of reality
Purpose—a deep, values-based belief that life is meaningful
Pivot—a strong ability to improvise

Perspective: Keeping It Real

Some might think that resilient people are those who are born positive or optimistic. And though some are prone to being extra cheery in times of trouble, or see the glass as half full, that's not always the case. Having a realistic perspective about your situation is key to building resilience. If you find yourself in the middle of a tough situation and you are aware of what is at stake, you're in a great spot! In urban vernacular, we would say "keeping it real," meaning we are being completely honest with ourselves and others.

If you find yourself wading in the waters of denial, that is a coping mechanism. *This will all blow over. Tomorrow is a new day. I'm going to put my head in the sand until the storm passes.* To have a realistic perspective, we all must do the hard and tiring work of being honest about what is going on in our lives, while still believing in a hopeful end.

Pizza Case Study

Perspective: We faced a hungry group of older kids who wanted to steal our pizza.
Perspective: We were outnumbered and there was a chance we could get beat up.
Perspective: We had to decide what was worth risking.

My dad, a Marine Corps corporal and Vietnam veteran, would often recount stories from war. He had an uncanny ability to identify who would be the first to cry or want to quit during training. In similar fashion, Admiral James Stockdale fought in the Vietnam War and discovered certain characteristics of soldiers who broke the fastest (from mental breakdowns all the way to death) while observing fellow prisoners of war (POWs). He inspired the term *Stockdale Paradox* based on those who didn't have a realistic perspective of their situation. They imagined they would be free within weeks. Then they hoped they would be free in months. When months turned into years, he realized that when his fellow POWs didn't survive, it was often because they imagined an unrealistic and unknown future. Stockdale *kept it real* and refused to slip into denial. In doing so, he remained unbroken as a prisoner of war for over seven years. Stockdale explained, "You must never confuse faith that you will prevail in the end—which you can never afford to lose—with the discipline to confront the most brutal facts of your current reality, whatever they might be."[2]

When life gets tough, grit is formed when you can see reality for what it is. Don't lie to yourself. You can't just slap a Bible verse on your problem and wish it away. You must maintain clarity about your reality, however uncertain, all while maintaining an unwavering faith that in the end, you will *more* than conquer.

Purpose: Making Meaning

Another ingredient to grit and resilience is the ability to make meaning in a mess. In other words, what do you have *now* to carry you through to the *future*? We've all heard the adage, "When life gives you lemons, make lemonade." Well, I want to expand this meaning-making into my future as well. So now when life gives me lemons, I'm not only making lemonade, but I'm also planting the seeds. Lemonade tastes good now, but I want to think about others who will need lemons in their future.

According to Coutu, "This concept was beautifully articulated by Viktor E. Frankl, an Austrian psychiatrist and an Auschwitz survivor. In the midst of staggering suffering, Frankl invented 'meaning therapy,' a humanistic therapy technique that helps individuals make the kinds of decisions that will create significance in their lives."[3]

We've seen this play out in countless lives, like the mother who lost her child in a drunk-driving accident and is now an advocate against drinking and driving. Or the financial coach who survived bankruptcy and now wants to help others understand the dangers of debt. Or the person who learned how to manage depression and now shares tips and techniques, offering hope to others who are struggling.

Pizza Case Study

Purpose: We protected our family's food and weekly celebration.
Purpose: We took a stand against bullying.
Purpose: We did not accept theft.

Let's be honest: we all know people who want to roll up in a ball, wallow in self-pity, and ask "Why *me*, God? *Why?*" (I've done this more times than I like to admit.) According to Coutu, "Such people see themselves as victims, and living through hardship carries no lessons for them."[4] But did you know that trials and hardships are necessary to living a life of impact? It's true. If you want to live a life worth living—one with meaning and purpose—it requires confronting pain, resistance, and fear.

What is the difference between those who are defeated by struggle and those who are sharpened by it? Between those who are broken by pain and those who are made wiser by it? Resilience. For us to blossom out of a seed of pain and flourish in wisdom, it requires resilience.

Pivot: Improvise and Adapt

The third building block of resilience is the ability to make do with whatever is at hand. But this isn't a one-and-done type of solution. *Pivot* is the repeated action of continually choosing to improvise, change direction, or adapt.

If this concept doesn't come easy to you, don't fret. I'll share a daily practice I learned as a kid that has built up my ability to pivot. Pivoting requires the ability to be inventive and improvise quickly. And since everyone has a kitchen and cooks in *some* capacity, all of us can build our ability to adapt.

Pizza Case Study

Pivot: We made the decision to prioritize getting home with dinner.

Pivot: We resisted the demands of the bullies.

Pivot: We made an escape route.

As a child in a large family living off one income, funds in our home were tight and we lived on a limited budget. We didn't have the luxury of wasting food. When I would look into the refrigerator and dramatically complain, "We have *nothing* to eat," my dad refused to believe it. I would stare at leftover chicken, a box of baking soda, and some random vegetables and call it *nothing*. My dad would see a full-course meal in the making. "Don't tell me you have *nothing* when you have *something*," he would retort.

When you have limited resources, become resourceful.

I learned this in the kitchen with my dad and it has manifested in all areas of my life. For example, my son came home from college after a delayed flight and was

> **When you have limited resources, become resourceful.**

ravenous as he dropped his luggage and went straight to the refrigerator. He lamented like the children of Israel stranded in the desert as he stared into the fridge, "All there is is chicken and cottage cheese?! We have *nothing* to eat!" This was my time to pivot and repeat the words of my father: "Don't tell me you have *nothing* when you have *something*."

Twenty minutes later, I had seasoned and grilled some chicken breasts with chipotle adobo sauce and spices, while I blended cream and cottage cheese to make a homemade alfredo sauce. I found bowtie pasta in the pantry that I boiled and added to the alfredo sauce, topped with the spicy chipotle chicken, and *bam*! Parker ate three servings of the pasta and now requests this dish from me every time he's home. When you have limited resources, become resourceful.

Friend, I want you to do the same thing. I want you to take random items in your fridge and make something delicious. This isn't about making you a better chef. This is about teaching you the simple art of adapting and improvising. I do this in ministry. I do this in creating. I do this in my marriage. Don't tell me you have *nothing* when you have *something*. Pivot.

The Cost of Resilience

We all want the benefit of being resilient or, at the very least, the ability to look back at failure and know we survived. Paul the Apostle wrote to the church in Rome during a time of trials, and in a rousing speech that would fire up any team at halftime, he shared the truth:

> What, then, shall we say in response to these things? If God is for us, who can be against us? He who did not spare his own Son, but gave him up for us all—how will he not also, along with him, graciously give us all things? Who will bring any charge against those whom God has chosen? It is God who justifies. Who then is the one who condemns? No one. Christ Jesus who died—more than that, who was raised to life—is at the right hand of God and is also interceding for us. Who shall separate us from the love of Christ? Shall trouble or hardship or persecution or famine or nakedness or danger or sword? . . . No, in all these things we are more than conquerors through him who loved us. (Romans 8:31–35, 37)

Oh, we love Romans 8:37, don't we? I mean, who *doesn't* want to be more than a conqueror? I read that verse, and I feel like Wonder Woman with her golden cuffs and shiny lasso. I'll take on anyone and shout, "I'm a conquering warrior! No, I'm *more* than a conqueror."

The problem with that sentiment is that we want to be conquerors, but we don't want to conquer anything.

We want to be overcomers, but we don't want anything to overcome.

Make no mistake about it: there is a cost to victory, and resilience requires sacrifice.

> There is a cost to victory, and resilience requires sacrifice.

If you read Romans 8 in its entirety, you'll see that Paul encouraged us that our suffering in the present pales in comparison to the glory of eternity. But he didn't ignore the pain of the suffering either.

What we see in this brief—but powerful—statement are the requirements of resilience:

Perspective
Purpose
Pivot

Just look again at the words of Paul to the Romans: "What, then, shall we say in response to these things? If God is for us, who can be against us?" (8:31). If that isn't *perspective*, I don't know what is. We may battle, and we may suffer, but we aren't alone. Through the presence of the Holy Spirit, we are not alone. He takes our deepest needs and painful prayers—even the prayers we can't utter—and relays them to God. The Holy Spirit intercedes for us (vv. 26–27).

In our waiting—and even our wondering—we can be confident in one thing: God is for us. In Paul's words to the Romans, he told them that God is working out every circumstance for good. Those words weren't just for the Romans, they are for us today. God chose us before we knew Him and destined us to be called, justified, and glorified (vv. 28–30).

That is our *purpose*. We have been destined to live a life worthy of the call of Christ. What does that mean? You were made on purpose, with a purpose, for a purpose.

When Paul encouraged us with the truth that God is for us, that means nobody can make an accusation against us and make it successful. No matter what the Enemy tries to throw at you—accusations that you are a failure, temptations to quit, or even poor decisions made in frustration or sadness—Jesus intercedes for us. He paid for every mistake, failure, and sin with His own blood (vv. 31–36).

This is the *pivot*! We start reframing and getting creative about how we view our circumstances. Sure, you lost your cool and screamed loud enough that your deceased great-aunt heard you from the grave say, "Screw this! I quit." Or maybe you've been tired of waiting for the thing you've been praying for, so you made a bad decision, acted on impulse, and are left with the repercussions. Or you repeatedly have gone back to bad choices, relationships, or friendships out of desperation and loneliness.

No matter how terrible or powerful our mistakes and failures, nothing can ever separate us in any way from God's love for us in Christ (vv. 38–39). Nothing, *nada*, zilch! Whatever we face—trauma, trial, or tribulation—we can persevere.

One person plus God is an unbeatable equation.

You are more than a conqueror because your resilience is not your own. You have the power of the resurrected Christ residing in you.

Perspective. Purpose. Pivot.

Don't let anyone steal your pizza.

THE NITTY-GRITTY

Principles

- If you never envision the end, you'll give up in the middle.
- Celebrate the small, daily wins. You're doing this!
- Perspective: Maintain clarity about your reality, however uncertain, while maintaining an unwavering faith that in the end, you will *more* than conquer.
- Purpose: If you want to live a life worth living—one with meaning, impact, and purpose—it requires confronting pain, resistance, and fear.
- Pivot: The repeated action of continually choosing to improvise, change direction, or adapt.
- When you have limited resources, become resourceful.
- There is a cost to victory, and resilience requires sacrifice.
- You were made on purpose, with a purpose, for a purpose.

Paul's Wisdom

"And we know that in all things God works for the good of those who love him, who have been called according to his purpose. For those God foreknew he also predestined to be conformed to the image of his Son, that he might be the firstborn among many brothers and sisters. And those he predestined, he also called; those he called, he also justified; those he justified, he also glorified." (Romans 8:28–30)

Prayer

Heavenly Father, thank You that I'm more than a conqueror in You. Remind me that with Your power residing in me, I can do whatever You've called me to do. Reveal Your purpose in me! Show me what You want me to do. Whatever sacrifice is required of me, let me step into my calling with confidence and joy. In Jesus' name, amen.

chapter four

THE INVITATION

*You were running a good race. Who cut in on
you to keep you from obeying the truth?*

PAUL THE APOSTLE (GALATIANS 5:7)

The invitation to go deeper into your strength and tenacity will cost you something. But you are worth the price. I don't know exactly what you're going through. However, I'm almost positive I know the *feelings* you're feeling. Let me take a stab at it:

You are exhausted and want to give up. Every step forward feels like you won't make it to your next. You are so tired throughout the day, but when your head hits your pillow, your mind wanders to places of escape and to worries about tomorrow.

You feel hopeless and think nothing will ever change. You fight for faith and believe with every new day possibilities of change loom. But by the end of the day, you have lost motivation and feel like this season will be your forever.

You feel like the clock is moving forward while your life remains stagnant. *Tick, tock. Tick, tock.* Do you hear it? Yeah, it's the hands of time reminding you that your days, weeks, months, and years are escaping you. You're still in the same job; you're still in the same house; you're still driving the same car.

You feel like you made a bad choice and now have to live with the results. If you would've picked a different college, you would've gotten a better job. If you didn't get pregnant, you would've had freedom. If you didn't move to that new city, you might have had better relationships. If you didn't choose that job, you would've been promoted by now. If you didn't marry your spouse, you would've been happier.

You feel stuck and unable to find a way out. No matter what you have done, no matter what classes or trainings you've participated in, no matter how many therapy sessions you've been through, you feel absolutely stuck. You are looking for the corner of a circular room—it's pointless.

I get it. I've been there. The previous examples aren't simply from my imagination or what *you* might be feeling. They are pulled straight from the toughest moments of my own life. Over the past decade specifically, I've felt exhausted physically, hopeless relationally, stagnant professionally, and stuck emotionally. And the downward cycle ends with the thought that my life is a result of all my poor decision-making. Throw me a pint of ice cream, and

I'll dive into it as though the answer to all my problems is at the bottom of the carton.

But hear me very clearly: you have a choice.[i] Yes, you have agency over your life. You will decide if you want to continue this journey or if you will quit. You'll either choose to grow your resilience and cultivate grit or walk away.

The payoff isn't always a medal or an award. You aren't guaranteed first place, a victor's crown, or a wedding ring for persevering. So why do we push forward? Why not just throw in the towel and walk away?

For some, the prize of resilience is standing and knowing whatever force, opposition, or challenge didn't take them out. Those are the people who run marathons *for fun.*

But for the rest of us, it could be so much more.

> **You will decide if you want to continue this journey or if you will quit.**

For me, grit isn't about testing my will or achieving success. Yes, knowing your *why* and refusing to quit is wildly important to being gritty. Purpose is integral to perseverance. But if I had to narrow down these concepts and give you the overarching reason as to why I refuse to quit, it's this: I press forward because I want to obey. I'm still here out of nothing more than obedience.

As a kid, I felt like obedience was punishment. Now as an

---

i. Before you make any crazy decisions and quit, I firmly believe you have an option to make the right choice. In the appendix, I wrote about the five critical questions you need to ask before you walk away. Make sure you check out those nuggets of wisdom!

adult, I understand obedience is the greatest act of love. So many times I've wanted to throw my hands in the air and give up. I've had legitimate reasons to quit and walk away. It wasn't will or strength that kept me going; it was obedience. Out of love for my God and obedience to His will, I knew I had to keep going.

> Have you heard of Noah? He was an Old Testament hero who was told to build an ark, which, keep in mind, no one had ever seen or heard of prior to this (and also note Genesis 7 hints that it had never rained on the earth before). Noah continued to build the ark for years upon years in the face of mockery. Everyone thought he was crazy.
>
> Until it started to rain.
>
> The ones who laughed at him, mocked him, and scoffed at him were the ones who were now asking Noah to save them by allowing them on his ark.
>
> *Grit* is unwavering obedience even when it doesn't make sense how to get there or how it will end. (And with perseverance, even the snail made it onto the ark!)

Pastor and theologian Eugene Peterson coined a phrase that beautifully encapsulates what it means to push forward. If I could define *grit*, *resilience*, and *perseverance* in one Peterson phrase, it's "a long obedience in the same direction."[1] Meaning, no matter what comes our way, we continue to press forward—no matter the obstacles.

And that's what this whole journey is about. Are we willing to obey, run our race, and not give up out of *obedience*?

You have a choice. You get to decide.

The Full Story

Remember the track story I told you in chapter 1? The one when I fell over hurdle after hurdle and limped across the finish line? Yeah, it wasn't a shining moment of glory, but it demonstrated grit in the midst of failure, pain, and embarrassment.

But there's more to the story. I told you what Coach Julia said. But let me provide alllllllll the details.

While I was in the first-aid tent being consoled by Coach Julia, she said, "I'm so proud of you! You didn't stop!" And for emphatic drama, she repeated herself and said, "You. Didn't. Quit."

In that moment, I instantly stopped crying and tilted my face toward her. Confused, I asked, "Are you telling me I *could've quit*?"

Friends, when I tell this story, I usually leave that part out. Why? Because it sounds so much more heroic that way. In fact, if a newspaper picked up the story, the headline would read: "Underdog MexiRican Stumbles Over Every Hurdle but Bravely Finishes Her Race!" I mean, that would be an article worth reading!

However, had I known I could've quit my race, I believe I would've walked off the track and given up. As I look back on that day and the conversation I had with my coach, I see how the experience shifted my perspective on every single challenge I have faced since. It has forced me to wrestle with the question, What if quitting isn't an option? Because, when it wasn't, I was pushed to persevere and complete the task set before me.

As it's been said, "Winners never quit, and quitters never win."

Paul the Apostle put it this way when he wrote to his friends in Corinth who were going through severe persecution and trial:

"Do you not know that in a race all the runners run, but only one gets the prize? Run in such a way as to get the prize" (1 Corinthians 9:24). *That* is my encouragement to you. Run to win (even if you are dead last and you've tripped over every hurdle). Run your race! Run to win! Run and don't give up!

> **If quitting isn't an option, then how will you proceed?**

This is the threshold, the decision to turn the page and continue the path of gritty resilience. If quitting isn't an option, then how will you proceed? It's a choice.

I chose "long obedience in the same direction."

If you're ready to get gritty, keep reading.

DISCLAIMER
When to Hold 'Em and When to Fold 'Em

The question you might be asking as you've been reading these chapters is this: *Is there ever an appropriate time to quit? Is it ever wise to walk away?*

The short answer is yes. There are times we need to shut down shop, leave an environment, and say, "No more." But a more comprehensive response requires a conversation. In the words of country legend Kenny Rogers, "You've got to know when to hold 'em and know when to fold 'em."[2] The following in no way covers all situations (wisdom and discernment are needed for personal problems), but here are some boundaries to help steer us in the right direction when it comes to quitting.

Abuse

If there is ever physical abuse—of any kind—then that is a clear signal to walk away. I have a hard line when it comes to physical touch, and if there is any kind of unwanted touch from a friend, spouse, coworker, boss, or your cousin's neighbor's mailman, you leave immediately. No one has the right to physically harm or inappropriately touch a person made in the image of God.

Emotional, psychological, and spiritual abuse are personal, so I leave boundaries up to you to figure out and define. Before you throw in the towel and write off your hurt feelings as *abuse*, I encourage you to commit to the journey of processing your emotions with a trusted counselor, therapist, or spiritual mentor.

Infidelity

I chose the word *infidelity* intentionally, and I want to be clear on the definition. I'm not specifically speaking in a relational context. This may apply to relationships, but I'm using *infidelity* with this definition: "unfaithfulness to a moral obligation."[3]

When we make deals, contracts, or covenants with people and someone breaks their word or is unfaithful in their promise, that could be fair grounds to quit. When promises are made, there is an assumption that all parties involved will fulfill the commitment. If someone doesn't maintain their word, what was contractually agreed upon is null and void.[ii]

We are currently living in a time where obligation is fleeting and ephemeral. If you make a promise, you can break it. If you say yes, you can easily just say no. Obligation is anything but that! Obligation binds us to a person or a project. It arises out of an authentic and genuine sense of duty, and in a culture that, more and more, prioritizes personal delight, it is crucial that we maintain clear sight on the importance of being true to our word.

Rest

There are seasons where we can still be in our marathon race, but we slow down or walk. Maybe we even take a break. When we talk about grit and resilience, there is an undercurrent of movement. However, this is based on your season and determining whether this is a momentary break to heal or catch your breath. Rest is part

---

ii. Note to my mother: See, Mom! All those years of watching television dramas about lawyers and contracts is coming in handy.

of resilience! Though this book is focused on the forward movement and learning how to build grit, I wholeheartedly believe rest is part of our advancing forward.

Here are some resources that have helped me on my journey to becoming emotionally and spiritually healthy: John Mark Comer's book *The Ruthless Elimination of Hurry*, Peter Scazzero's *Emotionally Healthy Spirituality* (a book I've read three times), and *Leading on Empty* by Wayne Cordeiro.[4] We are all in this marathon together, but sometimes we need to catch our breath, and there is no shame in that.

Seasons

Change isn't synonymous with *quitting*, but sometimes change brings perspective. When life changes, we must reevaluate where we are spending our time, how we are spending our time, and what is changing with our investment of it.

Often when considering life seasons, we are prone to have an *on-to-the-next* mentality. We might purge people, ideas, and dreams too quickly—out with the old and in with the new. It's as if society makes us decide between one or the other. But that shouldn't always be the case. We need to embrace various seasons with curiosity and capacity, considering where and how we are spending our time and what is changing with our investment.

That being said, there are times when we need to be honest with ourselves. When reevaluating our lives in seasons of change, we might realize that nothing is wrong or broken or bad; the season is simply over. A friendship has run its course. A job has been completed. Priorities have changed.

I love the concept of holding the tension of *and*:

I'm moving to a new city, *and* I still connect with my girlfriends over Zoom.
I'm in a new job, *and* I still practice the lessons I learned in my old job.
I'm newly married, *and* I still make time to be alone.

You know a season has ended when both parties can celebrate an amazing completion while still holding the tension of being sad about transition. Finishing one season well is vitally important to thriving in the next season.

Now, let's get gritty and learn how to build grit and resilience!

GETTING GRITTY: HOW TO BUILD GRIT AND RESILIENCE

chapter five

THE
DIFFERENCE
OF A DECADE

"Did you receive the Holy Spirit when you believed?" They
answered, "No, we have not even heard that there is a Holy Spirit."

ACTS 19:2

Ten years ago, I sat on a maroon couch in a hotel lobby in Knoxville, Tennessee. Nervously running my hand along the fabric, one way and then the other, I watched the velvet material change color as my hand moved in each direction. *Swipe*, light side. *Swipe*, dark side. I was waiting for two conference organizers I had been asked to meet to discuss my session from the night before.

Not knowing what the organizers wanted to discuss, I ran through possible scenarios in my head:

Maybe they want to ask about my Bible cross-references . . .

Maybe they want to congratulate me on it being my first time
speaking at their event . . .

Maybe they want to invite me to next year's conference . . .

The possibilities seemed endless. My internal dialogue was
interrupted when both the leading pastors of the youth division of
this denomination sat across from me, a cherrywood coffee table
between us. The first leader took a deep breath, brushed invisible
dust from the table, and asked how I liked the conference.

"Between Louie Giglio, Francis Chan, and rapper Lecrae,
I'm humbled to even be invited to participate in any capacity," I
gushed. The arena had been packed. Ten thousand youth from
across America had journeyed to Knoxville for this conference.
Even all these years later, I can still tell you exactly what I taught
on, what I wore, and the words my mother prayed over me before
I took the stage.[i]

I was almost thirty years old and not totally sure what I was
called to do with my life. Don't get me wrong: I had the basics. I
had my master's degree. I knew I was going to marry Matt Olthoff.
I knew I loved Jesus and wanted to serve Him. I just didn't know
exactly how that was going to play out.

At the time, I was writing a blog and teaching Bible studies
at various youth groups and ladies' teas while volunteering in my
church's youth ministry. As a freelance writer and editor, I was
committed to creating content daily and was passionate about Bible

---

i. Yes, my mother was my travel assistant / prayer warrior / ministry buddy. It was
the first big event I ever taught at and—for all I knew—it could've been my last.
Might as well take my mama with me!

teaching. But on the heels of a seminary rejection,[ii] I wasn't sure if I was cut out for ministry or teaching the Bible.

Then I got an invitation to speak at a huge youth conference in Tennessee. I took it as a sign from God that maybe I was called to step into more of this.

The energy at the conference was electric. Worship music blared through speakers suspended high above the stage, and voices of the youth filled the space up to the rafters. It was a holy moment. I was nervous when I walked to the podium but preached with everything I had, from every fiber of my being. As I opened the Word of God, I felt my heart rate slow, and a calming peace washed over me. It was a moment like none I had ever experienced—I felt like I was in the center of exactly what God wanted me to do.

So imagine my confusion, in that hotel lobby the next day, when I, still high off the feeling, found myself face-to-face with conference leaders who looked . . . less than impressed. The leader speaking to me at the time pursed her lips together, eyes trained on mine, and cocked her head to the side.

Did I say something wrong?

She squinted and said, "We place a high value on education in our denomination. We know you didn't go to seminary, but why didn't you tell the students you at least went to graduate school? I appreciate how much Scripture you covered, but your references to pop culture seemed like a greater priority than referencing your theological foundation."

My breath caught in the back of my throat. I thought, *I use*

---

ii. This topic is for another book entirely, but in short, I was required to complete a preaching class in order to be accepted into the seminary program I had my sights on. The preaching class was offered only to men. So by default, I was kept out.

pop culture references because my goal is to make the biblical passages come alive in a way that resonates with my audience. And for what it's worth, I highly doubt a fourteen-year-old boy from Huntsville, Alabama, would've cared one bit that I have a master's degree in humanities with an emphasis in aesthetics.

I nodded as if I understood her, but I still didn't see where this was going. Her coleader piped in and said, "We knew we were taking a risk by inviting you, but we had hope. I'm not trying to be offensive, but we felt it was our obligation to inform you that your lack of biblical dexterity and formal education displays the weakness of your communication."

Took a risk on me? Not trying to be offensive? Lack of education?

I asked them if there was something theologically wrong with my message or if they thought I hadn't thoroughly explored the passage I was given. "Oh, there were lots of solid Scripture passages, and you did take us through the narrative, but these sessions are meant to be serious and the scholarship of our educators really matters to us," they said.

Their chief complaint? I made the kids laugh too much.

The conversation droned on, and I kept stroking the couch. *Swipe,* light side. *Swipe,* dark side. After twenty minutes, the organizers signed off, saying I had been entertaining and the students had loved the session. Unfortunately, YouTube Q&As and blog writing were all I was suited for because, you know, ministry is serious.

Thank you?

I stood, shook their hands, and smiled like I hadn't just been gut-punched. As I walked back to my hotel room, I felt like I had fast-drying concrete in my shoes; every step felt heavier than the last. When I got inside, my mom was on the phone talking to my pastor father about how proud she was of me. She pointed to the receiver, smiled at me, and waved. "She was a carbon copy of you," I heard her say. "So many young people came to know Jesus." I smiled at her and walked straight into the bathroom to sob.

I remember that feeling like it was yesterday. I can see my tear-stained reflection staring back from the bathroom mirror as I told myself I was never going to teach the Bible again. *I quit ministry.*

The feeling of ineptitude and failure was like a tattoo on my face. I was embarrassed and felt like everyone could see what I wanted to hide.

Ever been there? Maybe not in ministry, but fill in the blank with what you've said about your life:

I'm never going to do _____ again.
I'm too unqualified for _____.
_____ requires too much from me.
I'm never going to be able to _____, so why
   even try?

I get it. I really do. But maybe you feel like you are at the point where you can't give up because you know there's something more. You can't explain it. But inside you there is a shred of faith that believes this isn't where you stop; this isn't your final destination.

Along with many others, I call that a *holy hunch*.

A Holy Hunch Plus Godly Grit

Do you ever wish that God would speak from heaven in the voice of James Earl Jones and tell you exactly what to do? Me too.

Sometimes I just want the path to be laid out, simple, and neat. But life doesn't work like that, and neither does God.

When God speaks to me, it's never with a game plan, a blueprint, or a road map. More often than not, it's what is sometimes called a *holy hunch*. Though I don't hear the audible voice of God, the Holy Spirit leads me, guides me, and empowers me. Jesus promised us that He wouldn't abandon us; He would leave us an Advocate, the Holy Spirit, who will lead us and empower us to do things not in our strength but in His strength (John 14:16–21). The Holy Spirit is our guide and our comforter, and He gives us power.

> The Holy Spirit is our guide and our comforter, and He gives us power.

Maybe the reason that Peter said the Holy Spirit is a gift (Acts 2:38) is because having a guide and a comforter is literally the greatest gift in life. Why wouldn't everyone want this gift? This gift has the power to change our lives, yet so many Christians don't want or are unaware of the power we can possess as the people of God.

Why don't believers want the gift of the Holy Spirit?

1. Let's start with the fact that the Holy Spirit is referred to as a *ghost* or a *spirit*.
   a. Who wants to kick it with a ghost?
   b. That might feel foreign or even a bit scary!
2. The Holy Spirit is *unknown* to many.
   a. We fear what we don't understand.
   b. We fear what we can't control or explain.

3. The Holy Spirit in teaching and usage has been *manipulated* and *abused*.
   a. Maybe you've seen or heard or experienced something that wigged you out.
   b. I did and that's what made me terrified of even discussing the Holy Spirit.

I want to set the record straight: the Holy Spirit is not a ghost, not fire, not wind, and not a dove. He's often symbolized by these things, but they're not Him. The Holy Spirit is the third person of the Trinity. Not because He's less in value, but only because He's last to be revealed to us in the pages of Scripture. But all the greatness, grandeur, and glory that is in the fullness of God the Father is in the person of the Holy Spirit.

If you're a believer, that means that all the power, greatness, and authority of God is inside you. The Holy Spirit takes up residence inside your human spirit, and all things become new. This empowerment helps us live our lives with a *grit* given by the Spirit of God. Is there anything better?!

Don't feel bad for needing the empowerment of God's Spirit. In fact, the disciples themselves—who were mentored by Messiah, coached by Christ, and educated by Emmanuel—needed the power of the Holy Spirit. Jesus knew that if we're going to live life God's way, we need more than principles; we need power. We need more than education and information; we need assistance. This is the role of the Holy Spirit.

It was never God's expectation that God's people carry out God's principles without God's power. Let's get real: God's principles seem impossible without God's power.

You want me to love my enemies?
You want me to bless those who curse me?
You want me to forgive those who hurt me?
You want me to believe You are for me when everything else feels
against me?

God knows we can't do that without His power.

Jesus knew this and said, "And I will ask the Father, and he will give you another advocate to help you and be with you forever—the Spirit of truth" (John 14:16–17). Jesus essentially said, "I want to do more than just give you *hope*; I want to give you *help*."

When referring to the Holy Spirit, the three Greek prepositions used in Scripture that we translated to English are defined as:

alongside
in
upon

Why does this matter? Because the Holy Spirit isn't just a gift who is near us or within us. The presence of God can actually come *upon* us, like we see in Acts 2 at Pentecost. This *upon* encounter is what truly empowers not only the church as we see it today but Christians who lived empowered lives throughout history. When the Holy Spirit comes upon us, we are led, guided, and empowered to do what God calls us to do.

Is there a step-by-step manual for our lives? Nope. But when you have a Holy Spirit hunch, godly grit will help you make it through. When God speaks to us through His Holy Spirit, we can boldly step into our calling, adhere to a conviction, or run away from compromise. But *how* can we hear from God?

In the Old Testament, God spoke through burning bushes, donkeys, and clouds, and—truth be told—sometimes I want Him to speak to me the same way! I want a bird to descend and whisper to me in a sweet celestial voice, "It is I, God Almighty." We might feel like it was easier for the folks in the Old Testament because they had physical signs from God. But listen, friend, the people of the Old Testament *wish* they had what we have!

The only reason God spoke that way to people in the Old Testament was because

1. they did not have the closed canon of Scripture, and
2. the promise of the Holy Spirit given by Jesus was not yet displayed. (That's why the psalmist said in Psalm 51:11, "Do not . . . take your Holy Spirit from me.")

The Spirit of God was given to certain individuals in the Old Testament for a certain moment for a certain responsibility. When the task was over or they sinned, the Spirit left them. Thanks to the promise of Jesus, His Spirit speaks to us and helps us stay gritty and possess a power not to quit.

How to Hear from the Holy Spirit

We don't simply need God's voice to help us discern good and evil. We need His voice to discern between good and *almost* good. We need the voice of God to know His will versus our will. We need the voice of God to remind us we have the grit to keep going.

> **God doesn't speak to be heard. God speaks to be obeyed.**

And when God speaks, there's only one appropriate response: obedience. Like my dad always said, "Delayed obedience is disobedience." Any response other than obedience is an inappropriate response to the voice of God. God doesn't speak to be heard. God speaks to be obeyed.

So how do we hear from the Holy Spirit? As we take a look at Scripture, there are different ways people heard God.

Knowing

There are people who hear God through a deep sense of knowing. If you have a gut feeling or a deep conviction through intuition, don't dismiss it. That could very well be the Spirit of God talking to you. You might not be able to articulate what you sense, but it's a deep knowing. In Acts 16, we see Paul the Apostle had a deep conviction about taking Timothy on his missionary journey with him. Little Timmy wasn't the likely candidate, but Paul knew he was the one to go with him. We see the fruit of his knowing by the church and ministry that was the result of Timothy's life.

Knowers are awesome because they have deep convictions and will push through any barriers to accomplish what they intuitively know God is asking them to do. My husband, Matt, hears God through knowing. He gets a gut feeling, and very little will stop him from accomplishing what he *knows* God is asking of him. No matter how you sense God speaking to you, always go back to the Bible for confirmation. God's Word speaks to us.

Seeing

Perhaps you are someone who has spiritual vision. Maybe you have dreams while you're sleeping or visual images while awake. That could be the Spirit of God moving in your life. You might sense God through what you see. In 1 Chronicles 29:29, the Bible records the events of King David's reign, saying, "From beginning to end, they are written in the records of Samuel the seer, the records of Nathan the prophet and the records of Gad the seer." Whether through mental images or scenes in the mind, a seer has faith for the impossible and dedication to see it fulfilled. No matter how you sense God speaking to you, always go back to the Bible for confirmation. God's Word speaks to us.

Hearing

Maybe you hear God speaking to you. Whether it's an audible voice or a voice within, you know when God is speaking. In 1 Samuel 3:10, the young prophet Samuel heard from God directly: "The LORD came and stood there, calling as at the other times, 'Samuel! Samuel!' Then Samuel said, 'Speak, for your servant is listening.'" Whether it was an audible voice or something Samuel heard within, this is a beautiful example of God speaking to His children in direct ways.

In Acts 9:4–7, God also spoke directly to Paul. We know it was audible because the men who traveled with Paul heard it too. Hearers usually will hear things and use their own life or voice to communicate what God has told them. *Ahem*, I'll say it again because it bears repeating: No matter how you sense God speaking to you, always go back to the Bible for confirmation. God's Word speaks to us.

Feeling

Lastly, you might be the person who feels something empathically or physically. As a feeler, I used to dismiss these feelings as nothing more than a bad burrito I ate the night before. But as I've matured and learned how God communicates to me, I have embraced these feelings and know I'm sensitive to the things of God. In Psalm 22, we read powerful, prophetic prose penned by King David, and there's no doubt in my mind, he *felt* what he wrote. David *felt* words and penned the prophetic death of Jesus. And because feelings are fickle, I will say this again: No matter how you sense God speaking to you, always go back to the Bible for confirmation. God's Word speaks to us.

The Leading of the Holy Spirit

In Acts 13, we see the believers were worshiping and praying when the Holy Spirit came with specific instructions:

> While they were worshiping the Lord and fasting, the Holy Spirit said, "Set apart for me Barnabas and Saul [Paul] for the work to which I have called them." So after they had fasted and prayed, they placed their hands on them and sent them off. (vv. 2–3)

Um, excuse me? I have a lot of questions here. Sent them off where? With what connections? With what money? What was the plan? In Acts 13:4, we are told Barnabas and Saul were "sent on their way by the Holy Spirit." That sounds lovely and adventurous, but your homegirl needs a plan!

I've mentioned several ways already that the apostle Paul demonstrated godly grit. Here's another brilliant example. If you chart Paul's first and second missionary journeys, you begin to see how dependent Paul was on the Spirit leading him, guiding him, and protecting him. Paul wanted to visit some churches he planted in the region of Galatia, but we are told that he had a God-given vision to go to Macedonia. However, they were "kept by the Holy Spirit from preaching the word in the province of Asia" (Acts 16:6).

No matter what came Paul's way, he was sensitive to the holy hunch of the Holy Spirit.

And this? This right here? This makes all the difference.

In this section of the book, we are going to unpack what Paul's tools for success and survival were and what we can learn in our journey of following Jesus. Because no matter what you feel called to, if there is a divine assignment attached to it—like God asking you to start something, build something, or lead something—you will *definitely* need His Spirit to come upon you and empower you to go where you need to go and stay where you need to stay.

The reason I'm so passionate about allowing the Holy Spirit to lead us is because I know without a doubt I would've given up on ministry and serving Jesus a long time ago if I wasn't listening to the Holy Spirit.

A decade ago, after the heartbreaking meeting that followed my first big conference, I sat on the edge of the bathtub in a hotel bathroom vowing to quit ministry and get a job in banking. I thought ministry was too hard. What God asked of me was too much. I had nothing—not a mentor, not a seminary degree, not even an official job in ministry. But you know what I did have? I had a holy hunch. I felt the presence of the Holy Spirit and knew this wasn't the end of the road for me or what God was calling me to.

I had conviction, passion, and mustard-seed-size faith. The Spirit showed me I was meant to continue to use my words as weapons to help the people of God find freedom.

A Decade Later

I sometimes wonder what my life would've amounted to if I'd quit after that conference and walked away from my calling. I don't believe I would be cursed or forlorn by any means, but I do think about what my life might be like today if I'd listened to two seminary-educated pastors who told me I wasn't cut out for this.

Do I believe they had malicious intent? No.

Do I believe they thought they were protecting the body of Christ from the dangers of pop culture references and an illustrative way of teaching the Bible? Yes.

Do I believe they were trying to help by preventing me from pursuing a call they thought wasn't for me? Yes.

But they didn't have the final word on my life then, and they sure don't have the final word on my life now.

I say this not with pride but with Godfidence:[iii] I am called to preach the gospel with or without a seminary degree. I am called to serve others in ministry even though I am not a man. I am called to declare the truth of God's Word prophetically over the lives of people who may not even like me.

What about you? What business plan did you submit that was rejected and now you want to give up? What employer told you the

---

iii. God + Confidence = Godfidence

job was above you? What ex made you want to walk away from love? I'm here to whisper over you, "Don't give anyone the final word for your destiny."

The Holy Spirit wants to lead you, guide you, and empower you to do what you—and quite possibly everyone else—don't think you can do.

How do I know this? Well, the past decade has been filled with toils and trials, heartaches and heartbreaks. But through the power of God's Spirit, I haven't quit. I've written books, launched a podcast, started a prison ministry, planted a church with my husband, traveled all over the world to preach the gospel, and led more than thirty thousand people to accept Christ publicly as their Savior.

> Don't give anyone the final word for your destiny.

And if that wasn't proof enough, last week I preached the Word of God in an arena packed with ten thousand people. The energy at the conference was electric. Worship music blared through speakers suspended above the stage, and voices filled the air with worship up to the rafters. It was a holy moment. I was nervous when I walked to the podium, but I preached with everything I had, from every fiber of my being. As I opened the Word of God, I felt my heart rate slow, and a calming peace washed over me. It was a moment like many I have experienced before—I know I was in the center of exactly what God wanted me to do.

How did I know this? The Holy Spirit made it clear. The conference I was invited to speak at was in Knoxville, Tennessee—the exact city in which I was told ministry wasn't for me. Doesn't God have a funny sense of humor? Ten years of people telling me to quit, telling me I was unqualified, and telling me I was not educated enough to do what I'm currently doing, and God sent me back to the place where I said I was going to quit.

Know. See. Hear. Feel.

Trust God can speak to you, and have the courage not to quit.

Don't listen to haters. Listen to the Holy Spirit hunch.

THE NITTY-GRITTY

Principles

- God's principles seem impossible without God's power.
- The Holy Spirit is our guide and our comforter, and He gives us power.
- The Holy Spirit is not a ghost, not fire, not wind, and not a dove.
- If we're going to live life God's way, we need more than principles; we need power.
- We don't simply need God's voice to help us discern good and evil. We need His voice to discern between good and *almost* good.
- God doesn't speak to be heard. God speaks to be obeyed.

Paul's Wisdom

"So again I ask, does God give you his Spirit and work miracles among you by the works of the law, or by your believing what you heard?" (Galatians 3:5)

Prayer

Holy Spirit, thank You for being with me in my daily activities. Thank You for empowering me to do what is divinely asked of me. I ask that You continually fill me to overflowing with Your power, Your wisdom, and Your love. Come upon me for the miraculous and the mundane. Use me in new and powerful ways to walk in grit, and bounce back in resilience, and give me power to persevere. In Jesus' name, amen.

chapter six

RESISTANCE BREEDS RESILIENCE

*Anyone signing up for the kingdom of God has
to go through plenty of hard times.*

PAUL THE APOSTLE (ACTS 14:22 MSG)

F
ull disclosure: I spend a lot of my time somewhere between
living to my fullest potential and wanting to quit. The spec-
trum is wide, and some days are better than others. But that's where
most of us live. We aren't throwing in the towel; we're asking, Will
this even make a difference?

If we aren't careful, status quo will be our standard.

I'll do just enough to say I tried.
I'll say the words and hope for the best.

I will show up in person, even if my heart is far away.
I'll hide in my cubicle and watch the clock until it's time to go.

But your soul knows status quo is a no-go. There's more for you, and your soul knows it. If you do what you've always done, you'll stay where you've always been. That's not resilience; that's resignation.

Resignation is dangerous because it's almost always based in a legitimate loss or failure. No one resigns when everything is great. Resignation is rooted in some form of our current reality. This reality will cause us to fear hoping or believing that anything will change. This reality will ignite fear to dream or hope again. This reality will cause chronic disappointment. This reality will make us feel beat up and cause us to question why we should go on.

> **No one resigns when everything is great.**

Have you ever wanted to erase everything and start over? Just wipe the slate clean and have a fresh start?

Starting over can feel like an alluring solution, but it very rarely gets us where we ultimately want to be.

More often than not, conflict, challenges, and chaos offer us opportunities to evaluate where our problems are rooted. But discovering the root of a problem is both emotionally and psychologically demanding. It takes time and patience and a gritty commitment to the greater goal. Quite frankly, it's hard work! This is why it's so appealing to simply wipe the slate clean.

If I just quit my job, then I will be truly happy.
If I just move to a new city, then I will be able to find real
friends.

If I just get married, then I will be able to start my life.
If I just get divorced, then I will be free to find my truest self.

Or consider these less-sweeping ideas that can be just as powerful at keeping us stuck:

If I just eat the chocolate cake, then I will be happy.
If I just watch one more episode, then it'll be enough.
If I have just one more glass of wine, then I will stop hurting.
If I just buy that designer purse, then I will feel like I fit in
*   and belong.*

But is a new job, new purse, new spouse, or no spouse the answer? Not likely.

Most of the time, when we struggle, it's within the framework of the choices we believed were the best ones we could make. To translate that into Christianese, we were obeying the God-call on our lives. You said yes to your job, you said yes to the move, you said yes to serving at church, and you said yes to your spouse. You did what you felt led by God to do. *So why is there so much resistance?*

Paul the Apostle was called and anointed. Charged to spread the gospel, he preached and taught everywhere he went. Powerful revivals began breaking out, and people received salvation. In addition, Paul facilitated miraculous healings. In Acts 14, we see Paul and Barnabas boldly preaching the gospel in Lystra. While there, Paul supernaturally healed a paralyzed man who hadn't walked since birth. Invoking the name of Jesus, Paul commanded the paralyzed man to get up and walk, to the shock of crowds of witnesses. The astonished onlookers began to worship Paul and Barnabas, calling them Zeus and Hermes, Greek gods in human form.

Paul was dismayed at the people's misappropriation of the miracle. He insisted that it was God's power, not his own, that had healed the man. But even after his explanation, the crowd *still* insisted on offering sacrifices to Paul and Barnabas. When a group of religious Jews managed to gain control of the frenzied crowd, they stoned Paul.

So what happens when you are doing what you have been called to do and you get knocked down *because* of it? What if you are persecuted? What is your move when stones are being thrown at you (granted, not real stones, the way it was for Paul, but proverbial stones of hatred)?

This kind of resistance can stop us in our tracks.

Paul was stoned, dragged outside the city gates, and left for dead. Though I can safely assume few of us relate to an experience quite that extreme, I believe we can all understand what it's like to feel beat up when we're pursuing God's call on our lives.

Falling from Trucks and Rising in Prison

When I tell you I injured my ankle jumping from a moving truck, it sounds dramatic, doesn't it? Like I was escaping vicious kidnappers and courageously rolling between speeding cars on the highway in order to, at last, hobble victoriously off to freedom. But let me clarify: it was a U-Haul. It was technically a moving truck, but it was most definitely not moving.

One Sunday afternoon, after packing up our newly founded mobile church into trucks, I Tetris-ed the last of our overfilled plastic bins into place. Satisfied, I walked to the edge of the truck bed to hop off. When I landed, I somehow rolled my ankle. I fell to the ground, writhing in pain.

I lay on the hot, black tar of the parking lot as my face burned and my ankle throbbed. I screamed for Matt, who rushed over to pick me up and carry me inside. I sobbed in pain as he assessed the situation. "I need to go to the hospital and get X-rays," I told him. "I think I broke my ankle."

Matt said that he could take me, but he gently reminded me that I was supposed to get on a plane and fly to Texas to host a women's conference in a prison the very next day.

I didn't think I could cry louder or with more ferocity, but in that moment, I lost it. The pain moved from my ankle to my heart. On the filthy floor of our rented church venue, I sobbed and sobbed.

I had spent months planning this event, and it was the first time we were granted access to host a conference for men as well as women. In total, we had plans to host not one, not two, but *three* conferences. I had both raised and personally funded thousands of dollars to make this event possible, and now I might not even be able to go to the conference.

Suddenly I was consumed by the all-too-familiar feeling that even as I was trying so hard to do what was right, everything was still going wrong. I really wanted to move forward, but after all it took to get this far, my sudden injury felt like the last straw. There was too much resistance for me to (literally *or* figuratively) get back up.

Eleven hours in the hospital emergency room, six X-rays, and a bottle of painkillers later, I left the hospital on crutches, diagnosed with a bad sprain. I was at my wits' end. Though the pills had me a little loopy, I was still in pain and told Matt we needed to cancel the event. *Who cares that we already paid for the catering? Who cares that there are volunteers flying in? Who cares if months of planning will have all been for nothing? I don't want to do it; I don't want to go.*

I can't blame the meds I took for that explosion of emotion. When I look back on that day in the context of the season I was in, I wanted any excuse to walk away. *Serving Jesus shouldn't be this hard*, I told myself. For Pete's sake, I wasn't serving the incarcerated for popularity or wealth. I was going into prisons because inmates needed to know that they could experience true freedom even while in prison.

The pain in my ankle was sudden, and in that moment, it was clear and present. But even bigger than the sprain was something in my heart that had been underscoring my day-to-day experience for months on end. Church planting—which, for the record, I did not *want* to do—came from my obedience to a holy hunch and had proven to be both draining and all-encompassing. The setup and teardown of everything needed for the church service, due to our lack of a permanent venue each week, was physically exhausting. Trying to build a team was taking an emotional toll.[i]

I watched pastors on social media, and their lives looked so easy, so full, and so abundant! Their gorgeous buildings must've been made possible by the many millionaires in their congregations. Their sermons must've come without effort, because clearly, they were way better preachers than I was. Their volunteer teams must've been overstaffed, because serving in *their* communities was somehow more rewarding. Other pastors seemed to lack nothing, while we were scraping by with what felt like a nickel and a wish.

Why was everything so hard?

---

i. To any church planter reading this book, I'm saying a prayer, wearing sackcloth, and lighting a candle for you. Rich are our rewards in heaven!

Matt took my crutches and placed me in our bed. He elevated my foot with a stack of pillows and said, "I'm not going to force you to do what you don't want to do. But what if this attack is the very thing trying to keep you out of prison?"

I went to bed that night and *knew* I had to get on that plane the next morning to head to Texas. This wasn't about me. This wasn't about the conference. This was about obeying and honoring the door that God had opened for me. There will always be resistance for those seeking freedom. There will always be resistance against you stepping into your calling, purpose, and potential.

And facing this resistance requires resilience.

Moving Past Resistance

In order for us to get a handle on how to move past resistance, we have to address our psychological ability to deal with difficulties and recover quickly. I'm not tired of saying it: we gotta be gritty. There are different tools we can employ when struggling against hardship. Here are four tools that can help us soar over life's hurdles with ease.

Insight

Insight is the ability to ask yourself tough questions when facing difficulties and give yourself honest answers in return. It represents the ability to face and accept the truth.

When we pause and look introspectively, we force ourselves to evaluate the motivations behind our choices, which can reveal the issues that have us stuck. Without strong insight, we can find ourselves naming the wrong solutions because we're not addressing the right problem.

Are you supposed to move to a new city, or are you just
running away from problems?

Are you supposed to quit your job, or are you feeling annoyed
with authority?

Are you supposed to end a friendship, or does their
accountability disrupt your lifestyle?

Are you in need of a new handbag, or are you trying to use a
label to prove your value?

If we don't rightly identify where our decisions are coming from, we will carry our brokenness from one season directly into the next. When we realize the root of the problem, the reassessment can begin.

> **Where does the root problem almost always lie? In ourselves.**

Where does the root problem almost always lie? In ourselves.

Please hear me: I'm not saying *you* are the problem. What I'm poking at is the hidden damage, offense, or trauma that is rooted in our past but manifesting in our present. My therapist always asks me, "What is the experience behind your reaction? What is the emotion behind the emotion?"

Misidentifying the answers to these questions will result in false fixes that may provide some amount of temporary relief but will ultimately leave you stuck to wrestle again and again with the same core issues.

Moving away from broken friendships won't heal your sense
of rejection.

Quitting your job won't remove your feeling of inadequacy.

Divorcing your spouse won't resolve your struggle with
intimacy.

Buying a material item won't sort out your sense of
unworthiness.

What's the emotion behind the emotion?

As I lay on my bed with my ankle wrapped tightly, I started to
ask myself why I was resisting the plan to host our prison outreach.
I realized chronic disappointment as a result of constant effort was
making me disappointed and disillusioned with God. The harder I
tried, the more failure I experienced. Where was this rooted? It was
the repeated effort I poured into church and feeling like the return
on investment paled in comparison to the effort I was putting in.
Where was this rooted? The feeling of inadequacy I experienced as a
child—no matter how hard I tried, I always felt like I came up short.

Once I realized I was having a pity party for one, I stared
at the ceiling and forced myself to articulate the decision all my
insight had led me to: "I'm going *despite* my feelings of ineptitude,
despite feeling crushed, *despite* all that has come up against me. This
opportunity doesn't come often, and I will make the most of every
opportunity I'm given, *despite* how I feel in a hard moment."

Independence

The way I'm using it here, *independence* refers to the ability
to distance yourself from the source of trouble in your life, both
emotionally and physically. It can also refer to the ability to distance yourself from outside influences or peer pressure as related to
decision-making.

When Matt settled me into our bed and started talking about
spiritual opposition, I believed him. But whether because of my

pride or my feelings toward God, I still didn't want to decide. I wanted someone (insert: Matt) to tell me what to do. But when we abdicate our own decision-making, it leaves us room to be mad at someone *else* if the result is anything less than what we would've wanted. Thankfully, Matt is a wise man. He didn't apply pressure or try to coerce me onto that flight to Texas. He knew when my emotions calmed down, I would make the right choice myself.

Other people can't be the power source to our resilience. Not only will we be prone to resent or blame them if anything goes wrong, but on the flip side, if things go well, we deprive ourselves of the grit-giving empowerment that comes from having made decisions independently.

In *God's Healing for Hurting Families: Biblical Principles for Reconciliation and Recovery*, David Thompson says resilience is the flip side of codependency.[1] Meaning, true resilience is fostered when an individual can make an independent decision for their own life and for their own good.

I woke up at four thirty in the morning, hobbled on my crutches into the car, and made my way to the airport. I made the independent decision to go to jail.

Relationships

When facing the hurdles of resistance, relationships are key in helping us build resilience. The beautiful detail of this ministry into jail was that since we had access to host a men's conference, too, I had invited my dad to join me. So together with my dad, I was able to have a relational connection in a moment of frustration. Not only was my dad there to teach during the sessions in the conference with me, but he also became my personal wheelchair chauffeur and carted me around the airport, the hotel, and the jail.

Without the relational help of my dad, I know the trip would've been so much harder to pull off.

Creativity and Humor

Did you know creativity and humor are related to resiliency? You might not think playing or laughing are part of resilience and grit, but they are!

> *Does it seem wrong to daydream about a beach vacation at a doctor's appointment?*
>
> *Would it be inappropriate to laugh when you have a flat tire?*
>
> *Is it problematic to draw or doodle during a stressful work meeting?*

It's not! These are tools of resilience. You're using creativity and humor to propel yourself through challenging moments that might otherwise have nearly knocked you over.

Back to the busted-ankle saga: We arrived in Texas, and my dad wheeled me to our rental car. We needed to pick up some last-minute supplies for our conferences, so I decided to take advantage of our trip to Walmart by investing in some deliciously tacky gold sequin. I figured if I was going to have to hobble into this jail feeling dorky and vulnerable, I might as well do it in a gold-studded foam bootie. And since my taste in fashion has always dwarfed my budget for fashion, I decided I wasn't just decorating my boot; I was going to *design* it. Inspired by one of my favorite Italian fashion houses, and firmly rooted in my ghetto-fabulosity, I neatly aligned the gold studs to spell out B-i-a-n-c-i-a-g-a on the inside heel of the bootie (instead of Balenciaga; it was the Bianca-version of it).[ii]

---

ii. Note: The desire to own Balenciaga was *before* their decision to exploit children

Friend, if you can't laugh at yourself, no one will. My gold-studded boot and I rolled into jail like a diva, big as the Texas sky.

It's so clear to me now the way creativity and laughter were the tools that fueled my resilience through what had—just a single night before—seemed utterly impossible to navigate. By my rolling up to the jail in my wheelchair and crutches, it was an act of resilience. Simply showing up was my act of retaliation against the Enemy. Let's not get it twisted: there is opposition against the gospel and the freedom the Word of God brings. Jesus referred to our Enemy as a thief who wants to "steal and kill and destroy" (John 10:10). So the very fact that I made it to Texas was like my soul screaming out, "Bump you, Satan! You tried to take me out, but I'm still here, sucker. Even if I have to hobble, wheel in, or drag my butt into this jail, you won't stop me. In the words of the rapper DMX, 'Get out the way!'"

Resilience Requires Resistance

You can't be resilient without experiencing resistance. This might seem defeating, but it's true. I need you to know there is always a cost attached to the decision to persevere. But can I also tell you there is huge reward?

In Acts 14, Paul was stoned for performing a miracle and preaching about Jesus, then he was dragged out of the city to die. When the other believers finally found Paul, they circled around him, and something unexpected happened. Acts 14:20 records that Paul miraculously stood up. Hang on. *Hold up.* Friends, Paul

---

in their controversial 2022 ad campaign. I will stick to my regular ol' shoes and be proud of staying on budget.

the Apostle wasn't just beaten up. The Greek word used in this verse to describe Paul getting up is *anistemi*. That word is used in the New Testament for people being raised from the dead or standing up.[2]

But it doesn't stop there.

Paul miraculously got up from

> You can't be resilient without experiencing resistance.

the brink of death and then went *back* to the city from which he was dragged out. You know what I think Paul was communicating by going back into the city? The ultimate message of God's power. I can picture him saying, "Bump all y'all! You tried to kill me, *but I'm baaaaaack*! I raised a paralyzed man from the floor, but God raised me from the dead! Get out the way!" Resilience always requires resistance.

For me personally, I need to know that something can be done. If I see someone like Paul take a licking and keep on ticking for Jesus, then I can too. If I see Peter build the church amid persecution, I can too. If I see James write a letter of faith to those persecuted because of their faith, I can too. If I see Paul and Silas worship while incarcerated, I can too. If I see Lydia build a business and give her profits to fund ministry, guess what? I can too.

When I finally arrived in that jail, I knew that there was a company of spiritual family who had gone before me—and a company of spiritual family who had gone with me that day—to do what so many others have done before: worship God no matter the circumstances.

The conference was truly amazing—one of my favorites, in fact. During worship at one point, a tall inmate with chocolate skin and short braids approached me. She asked me if she could sing.

If I'm honest with you, my first thought was to issue a resounding no. I didn't know who she was, what she would say, or if she could even sing. But when a six-foot-one inmate in prison attire asks you for the microphone, the answer is always yes.

The room went quiet as a holy hush fell over the prison pod. Mia closed her eyes and began to sing a sweet melody about Jesus being her defender, Jesus being her protector, and Jesus bringing justice. Her insight was part of her resilience. The women in the room clearly resonated with what they were hearing, and they started nodding in agreement. Clearly Mia's faith was independently her own, but she fostered relationship with the women in her prison pod and was now leading them. Her relationships were part of her resilience. When the hook of the song started—a chorus that was simple and true—Mia freestyle-rapped over the music, "It's just me and Jesus! It's just me and Jesus!" She encouraged us all to repeat the words with her. "It's just me and Jesus! It's just me and Jesus!" We all stood to our feet with laughter and applause as she hyped us up like Chance the Rapper. "It's just me and Jesus! It's just me and Jesus!" Mia refused to resign to the label of inmate. Her creativity and humor were part of her resilience.

I stood on my bedazzled Bianciaga bootie and hollered, "It's just me and Jesus! It's just me and Jesus!" We kept repeating it until the room worked into a frenzy and the prison guard had to calm us all down because it felt like a holy riot was about to go down. With joyous applause, Mia bowed like the queen of England in a formal curtsy and gave me the biggest hug I've ever received. Resilience oozed from this woman and left me drenched in hope.

Singing with Mia and being wrapped in her arms was a reminder that there will always be resistance to things that bring God glory. I recognize that her decisions and mistakes landed her in prison. However, she was using her time of incarceration to become the woman she knew God was calling her to be—a worshiper. Despite what her foster parents thought of her, despite what her teachers said she would never amount to, despite her family who said she would be in prison her whole life, she raised her voice and led the room in singing out a freedom song.

Freedom isn't free. There is a cost attached to calling, and hurdles are part of the race.

So cry and be angry, but then bedazzle your shoes and drag yourself back to the place that beat you up. There is work to be done, and you have been raised up to do it.

THE NITTY-GRITTY

Principles

- No one resigns when everything is great.
- There will always be resistance for those seeking freedom. There will always be resistance against you stepping into your calling, purpose, and potential.
- The four tools to move past resistance are insight, independence, relationships, and humor and creativity.
- When we pause and look introspectively, we force ourselves to evaluate the motivations behind our choices, which can reveal the issues that have us stuck.
- When we realize the root of the problem, the reassessment can begin.
- You can't be resilient without experiencing resistance.

Paul's Wisdom

"Anyone signing up for the kingdom of God has to go through plenty of hard times." (Acts 14:22 MSG)

Prayer

Jesus, thank You that You can resurrect me from moments that feel like death. When I'm beat up and dragged out of places where I'm misunderstood or simply don't want to be, will You remind me that I am resilient and that resistance is part of the plan? Give me Your insight in decision-making. Though I am independent from others, I want to be dependent on You. Be my strength and help me forge and foster the right relationships. Give me creativity to find ways to express myself when words fail me, and let me laugh at mistakes instead of cry. Even when I'm frustrated or feel like a failure, help me think of others more than myself. These will be my brave and bold acts of resilience in the face of resistance. To You be the glory, amen.

chapter seven

TRAIN YOUR BRAIN

Do not conform to the pattern of this world, but be transformed
by the renewing of your mind. Then you will be able to test and
approve what God's will is—his good, pleasing and perfect will.

Paul the Apostle (Romans 12:2)

We've all been there, right? You missed the alarm, overslept, and now you're going to be late to work. You don't have time to wash your hair, and—as you commonly do—you forgot to put the laundry into the dryer. *Forget it! I'll just have to rewash the entire load of mildew-smelling clothes when I get back.* As you pack up your purse, your laptop, and your oat milk latte, you realize you don't have your keys. Oh, but it gets worse: you don't know where your keys are. The feeling goes from rushed to rage! As you look for your lost keys in drawers and handbags, the inner critic gets louder and harsher:

Way to go, idiot.
You lost your keys again because you're a mess.
How could you be so stupid?
When will you get your life together?

Frustrations may seem inconsequential, but our responses to them create patterns in our brains. We may deal with smaller issues and move on, but when a larger or more traumatic event occurs, the ways we've trained our brains with the small stuff determines how we'll respond to bigger problems.

And while misplacing keys or sleeping through an alarm is frustrating, there undoubtedly will be more serious situations that aren't just inconveniences. Whether it's an untimely death or devastating divorce, addiction or infertility, these will feel like attacks against our lives. We know how to survive the hiccups in life, but do we know how to survive the hurdles?

> **Frustrations may seem inconsequential, but our responses to them create patterns in our brains.**

When we feel like we are drowning in life or feel like we can't get up from an emotional blow, that's a sign our mental and emotional reserves are depleted. When we experience too many unsolved emotional aggressions or trauma, it can make us more prone to breaking down and less able to quickly recover.

How in the world do we bounce back from situations like these? You guessed it: by developing grit and strengthening our resilience.

As we will discover, scientific research has demonstrated that resilience and grit are behavioral outcomes of a mature, well-functioning prefrontal cortex in the brain. As we know from the research of Dweck and others, we can retrain our brains.[1] It's going to require work, but the good news is grit is gettable. Yes, you read that right. Grit is something you can acquire.

Your Thoughts, Amygdala, Prefrontal Cortex, and the Choke Hold

This is your warning: our discussion will require you to put on your thinking caps.[i]

We are going to do a light dive into the deep topic of neuroplasticity and the brain pathways we can strengthen to build resilience. This will get science-y (clearly, I'm very technical with my choice of terminology), but please don't tune out or skip this chapter. This will help us understand the brain function behind wanting to give up or run away when we face difficulties.

I'm not a neuroscientist, but about seven years ago, I began a personal counseling journey. I really wanted to explore mental health and learn how I could heal from past trauma in my life. Get ready to weave Scripture and science together to help us train our brains to bounce back from failure, loss, and trauma.

It's time for the nitty-gritty.

Let's start with some basics. God is a masterful designer and creator. He designed each of us with an almond-shaped mass

---

i. My mother always used the phrase "Put on our thinking caps" when we were going to learn something that required mental focus. It's still so weird, but now I say it. You can steal it.

known as the *amygdala*, which is the part of the brain that's hard-wired for survival.

Your amygdala is a gift from God! If you ever find yourself in a moment of fight-or-flight, that's a sign your amygdala is actively engaged. Any time you're in danger or perceive a threat, the amygdala kicks in and sends your body strong doses of adrenaline.[2] Think of it like a neon sign that pops up and warns you, "Watch out! Be on guard! Be alert! Run if you have to!"

See a shark while you're peacefully snorkeling?

See a car speeding toward you that's a little too close for comfort?

See a hulking stranger while all alone in a dark parking lot?

You better believe your amygdala is in high gear.

God gave us the amygdala for our protection, but it is not discerning. It's built to protect, and it's very easily triggered.

Quick example of what I mean here.

When I was five years old, our house was broken into. My mom and I were the first ones on the scene, and I saw the busted door and the disaster just beyond. It was Christmastime, and our beautifully decorated home was now in complete disarray. The tree had been toppled, the presents were gone, and our holiday food had been stolen.

All these years later, if I close my eyes and think about that moment, I can feel the tension in my body rise. My pulse increases, and a jolt of energy runs through my veins. The memory triggers the exact same part of my brain that the experience did. My amygdala is screaming, *Be careful! Be on guard! Be ready to run!*

Thankfully, our on/off amygdala doesn't have to do it alone. God gave us the ability to employ logic from the part of our brains called the *prefrontal cortex.*[3] This way, if you hear a noise at night and the amygdala screams, *Someone is breaking into your house! You're gonna die!* the prefrontal cortex can step in and tell you, *It's probably the wind. You're fine. There's very likely a logical explanation.*

The amygdala is all panic. The prefrontal cortex is all logic.

The amygdala responds according to the preprogramming. In other words, if you had an awful experience with a home invasion, you might tend to believe every knock at the door is another burglar trying to break in. (Yes, I'm fully aware that a burglar wouldn't knock before breaking in, but again, the amygdala isn't logical.)

And I don't know what it would be in your life, but because of some hurt or trauma or even a misunderstanding, my guess is that there are certain people or places that trigger feelings of anxiety and fear and tension in you. The prefrontal cortex can regulate a raging amygdala with logic. You can train your brain so that you can stay better regulated. And when you need more than your own logic because you are challenged by too much to handle in your own strength, guess what else you can tap into? Divine power.

Without even knowing it, your mind can race to a worst-case scenario, where you find yourself short of breath and panicking, trying to control things you can't control, completely overwhelmed by a runaway mind. That's why Paul the Apostle told his friends and fellow believers in Corinth,

For though we live in the world, we do not wage war as the world does. The weapons we fight with are not the weapons of the world. On the contrary, they have divine power to demolish strongholds. We demolish arguments and every pretension that sets itself up against the knowledge of God, and we take captive every thought to make it obedient to Christ. (2 Corinthians 10:3–5)

Paul told the Corinthians (and each of us who gets to read his letter) that we have divine power to straight *demolish* strongholds. Not only that, but we can "take captive every thought." Every time I think something I shouldn't think,[ii] I have divine power given by God to essentially get that thought and put it into a choke hold.

When I'm listening to my inner critic, when I'm sabotaging my own sanity, when I'm paralyzed by the lies ricocheting in my mind, I have to silence them by choking them out. Let's make this a visual flow:

I feel that I'm not enough → Identify my feeling

I want to quit → Identify my immediate reaction

I remind myself I'm called, chosen, empowered, and I'm choosing obedience → Combat the reaction with the truth (basically, get those lies in a headlock and choke them out until they are silent)

Sounds aggressive, right? But stay with me: we have the divine power to choke out the lies the Enemy is whispering to us and to destroy the pathways in our brains that aren't healthy. Paul was reminding us that we don't have to wage war like the world does

---

ii. *I'm a failure! I'm a loser! My life will never change! My life will always be this way!* And all the other devastating things we tell ourselves.

because our power isn't from the sword or spear. The weapons we yield have divine power to demolish strongholds.[iii]

So why do we worry? If we're followers of Jesus and we should completely trust in God, why is it that our minds often race in irrational ways? Why do we want to quit and give up when there is adversity? If these responses relate to past experiences, identify the hidden fears that motivate them. If they're spiritual attacks from the devil, combat the lies with the truth of the Word of God.

Whether the resistance is spiritual or rooted in trauma, we're experiencing an amygdala hijack. It is saying:

> *Your car payment is due on Friday, and you have no money in your account. You're in trouble.*
> *Your ovaries are drying up, and you haven't been on a date in years. You need to settle.*
> *Your dreams are slipping from your hands like grains of sand. You better take control.*
> *Your child can't read yet and is being held back an academic school year, which means he will inevitably fail before graduation and live a thug life on the streets selling drugs out of his car. You better work harder.*

Paul the Apostle realized the power of our thought lives, and that is why he encouraged us to "take captive every thought" and make it obedient to Christ. That's Scripture. When we weave that into the scientific standpoint, we need to tell our prefrontal cortex to grab the amygdala by its shoulders and say, *Get ahold of yourself! We're choosing to be spiritual. We're giving this to God.*

---

iii. Insert mental image of a Roman gladiator pounding his chest. Get pumped!

Three Practices to Build Resilience

Dr. Rick Hanson, professor of psychology at the University of California, Berkeley, argues that resilience training for your brain is like muscle building for your body. Strength is developed through lots of little efforts that add up over time. Little efforts throughout your day can result in real physical changes for a better brain.[4]

But the activation and integration of these practices are two different things. Hanson also says that there's some work to do between knowing how to be resilient and *being* resilient. Activating grit and resilience is temporary—it's possible to get gritty during one specific challenge and then revert to our old ways. But installing that habit into our brains—through consistent practice (put in those reps!)—will allow us to persevere for the long haul.

According to Dr. Hanson, you can teach your brain to be more resilient by working on these three practices to train your brain: self-compassion, mindfulness, and gratitude.[5]

Self-Compassion

My best friend, Melanie, repeats a phrase anytime she hears me speak negatively about myself, and it stops me in my tracks: "Stop talking about my best friend like that!" It's a sobering reminder that if I heard anyone talking about *her* that way, I would probably need to throw hands. And if I heard anyone else talking to *me* that way, we would, at the very least, not be friends. Yet I am harshly judgmental and lack the compassion for myself that I would dole out by the gallon to literally *anyone* else. Melanie's reframing allows me to see my own troubles and mistakes as part of being human.

As followers of Jesus, we know compassion should be extended to others. But do we extend compassion to ourselves? Instead of critical judgment, self-compassion is acknowledging our mistakes and faults and responding with kindness. Would you speak to a friend with the same harshness you speak to yourself?

There is a balance to this that must delicately lie between acceptance and improvement. Instead of highlighting mistakes or hiding in shame when failure hits, hold the tension between giving yourself and others grace, while acknowledging how things could improve. Kristin Neff, PhD, a pioneer in self-compassion research, identifies three main components of compassion:

1. Self-kindness: Remove the inner critic creeping in your mind and silence the negative self-talk with a kinder, more compassionate voice.
2. Common humanity: No one is perfect. We all fail and make mistakes. It's part of being human.
3. Mindfulness: Don't just take note of your negative emotions. Feel them, but don't react to them. Experience the feelings, but don't let the feelings rule you.[6]

Mindfulness

Mindfulness is a trendy word used from hip yoga instructors to TikTokers who teach breathing techniques to help center the mind. Though it might sound esoteric, it's really just being aware of what's happening as it's happening. In short, it's paying attention in the present moment. As followers of Jesus, our present moment is made fuller and more secure by knowing that God is present with us. Being mindful is being aware of what God's doing *now* and removes our attention to and preoccupation with *later*.

So train your brain! By consistently following healthy patterns

> **Being mindful is being aware of what God's doing *now* and removes our attention to and preoccupation with *later*.**

of thought, over time, your brain physically changes. Through the process of neuroplasticity, the brain forms new neuronal pathways to support this kind of thinking, even when you're not aware or trying to engage in mindfulness. Practicing mindfulness calms your brain and changes its default mode of operation.[7]

The best way I've found to incorporate this practice is whenever I use social media. In the last couple of years, I've experienced such division, hatred, and misunderstanding on apps that are supposed to be social. Whether I've been the target or someone else was a target for mean and caustic words online, I close the apps and do the following:

- **Pause and breathe.** Sometimes I just need to inhale and exhale to remind my amygdala that even though I might be experiencing fear or anxiety, I'm actually not being chased by a saber-toothed tiger and a burglar isn't at my door. *Breathe.* Focusing on your breath is an immediate path to mindfulness because it exists only in the present moment. There is no breath in a past regret and none in a future anxiety. Get present and breathe. Even thirty seconds of focused breathing can make a big difference.

- **Turn on awareness.** Judge if you want to, but I talk to myself and I'm not afraid to admit it. This practice has helped me become more aware of my reality. You don't have to talk aloud if that's not your thing, but get into the discipline of labeling the truth of your situation. State reassuring, logical facts—*I am safe*; *I am loved*; *I am kind*. This will wake up your prefrontal cortex.

- **Feel the feeling.** In a moment when my brain is hijacked and my neurons are going haywire, I give myself grace and compassion to feel the feelings. *I'm sad and feel lonely.* Or *I'm afraid I'll be taken advantage of again.* Or *I want to quit because I have failed at it so many times things will never change.* I give myself time to feel what I'm feeling. To really feel our feelings, we must be able to identify what's truly behind them.

  - Are you *sure* that you are feeling angry? Or is the emotion behind the rage simply sadness?
  - Are you *sure* you are feeling frustration? Or is the emotion behind the exhaustion really fear?
  - Are you *sure* you are feeling hungry? Or is the emotion behind the heaviness actually emptiness?

  And once you get down to the most elemental pieces of what you're feeling, *feel it*. It's okay to acknowledge your sadness, disappointment, or whatever else is going on—in fact, it's necessary.

- **State the truth.** No matter what we're feeling, there is always more to the story. When we are going down a path of wanting to give up and walk away, we need to take a holistic and balanced view of our situation.

  - *I'm sad and feel lonely, but I can call a friend or visit a family member because it will help me build community.*
  - *I'm afraid I'll be taken advantage of again, but this time I'm wiser and know better.*

- *I want to quit because success hasn't come yet, but with each failure I will learn something new that brings me closer to my goal.*

As a person of faith, I am privileged with a library of truths in God's Word. When I don't know what to think or I can't seem to identify a comforting truth, I lean on the teaching of my spiritual forefathers and foremothers and dig into Scripture. If I'm feeling overwhelmed or depressed, wanting to walk away and wither like a leaf, I remember God's Word, and His truth gives me strength.[8]

Mindfulness is a practice. It takes time and intentionality. But it has been proven—anecdotally by me, and scientifically by countless scholars—to help us live happier and more balanced lives.

Gratitude

Have you heard of *negativity bias*? It's a real thing. Science has neurological language and research to explain this, but I want the description to be simple. Think of negativity bias as Velcro for the bad thoughts and Teflon for the good thoughts. Velcro: bad thoughts stick. Teflon: good thoughts slide away.

Because of negativity bias, our brains attach to negativity. Positive things are harder to remember. It sounds kind of awful, but there's good reason for it. It's easier for our brains to process negativity.[9] So to prevent and restrain negativity bias, we must intentionally search and

> To prevent and restrain negativity bias, we must intentionally search and highlight the positive things in our lives.

highlight the positive things in our lives. We need to bring more awareness to the moments of joy we experience.

What do you feel?
What emotions can you identify?
What memory can you sear into your mind?

Do you want to know the one phrase that has proven benefits for both mental and physical health? It's *thank you*.[10] One study found that the practice of gratitude can increase happiness levels by an average of 25 percent.[11] And it's not even hard! Beneficial outcomes can be achieved by such simple practices as praying, writing in a gratitude journal, placing a thankful phone call, making a mental gratitude list, or writing a thank-you letter to someone.[12]

Pink Satin Top

Now let's put this into a real-life scenario that demonstrates how we can apply these practices to everyday challenges. This way, when big issues arise, we will know how to push forward and not quit.

Case Study: Pink Satin Top

Self-Compassion
Mindfulness
Gratitude

In the spirit of full disclosure, I've been in a season of weight gain, and it feels heavy. Writing those words is devastatingly hard for me, and not because my clothes don't fit or I feel like I've lost myself. It's hard because I literally don't know what else I can do to get where I want to be.

I'm dedicated to taking care of myself and putting in the effort it takes to be healthy. I work out six days a week, and I'm committed to working toward becoming faster and stronger every day.

I've always struggled with my weight. I was obese as a child and obsessed over weight loss in college. I gained weight when I got married and gained even more weight when we started the church. Even though I exercise and monitor my food intake, I still struggle to lose weight.

But don't get it twisted: being in a fluffy and Big Girl season doesn't mean I have given up on trying to look nice, okay? In fact, sometimes it feels like I have to work twice as hard to feel half as good. (Is that too honest for you? I can't help but be real right now.) This past weekend at church, I really wanted to put in effort. I bought a new top: a bright fuchsia-pink satin top with a cutout between the shoulder and neckline. I call it *conservative sexy*—a little skin, a lot of color. I was feeling confident and wore my hair in a sassy high ponytail to complete my look.

In true Bianca fashion, just as I was leaving for church, I noticed a small stain on my brand-new top. I was rushing to get out of the house, so I spot-cleaned it and ran out the door. What I learned the hard way is that satin doesn't clean up so easily. In fact, my attempt to get rid of the stain made it flower into, you guessed it, an even bigger stain. When someone at church mentioned it, I tried to hide my faux pas by tucking the shirt into my favorite jeans.

But you want to know what a woman who's self-conscious about her waistline should never do? She should never tuck in her shirt to hide a stain, because that will highlight said waistline and send her self-consciousness (I promise, she's working on it!) into overdrive.[iv]

I knew I was going to be on camera, which, of course, adds ten pounds (strike one); I would be seated (strike two); and I'd be in a position where all my rolls would be highlighted (strike three, batter! You're out).

When I saw the video content online, my soul shattered from embarrassment. My first thoughts were: *You are so fat, and you look horrible. That was the absolute worst outfit! Why do you even bother? You should only ever wear all-black muumuus, sister. It's time to give up trying.*

Step One: Self-Compassion

After my mini meltdown, I took a couple of breaths and decided to *choose* self-compassion. My inner critic doesn't have an inside voice, and she can be absolutely deafening. But instead of automatically dissolving to self-hate, I lovingly shushed that broad and changed the dialogue:

Bianca, you have been working so hard. Your body is grateful for your food choices and exercise routines. It's easy to point out all the soft and squishy parts of your body, but don't forget the strong and awesome parts of you. Like, your winged eyeliner was so fierce it could've sliced something! And you aren't alone in this struggle. Many men and women feel insecure with their bodies. Instead of

---

iv. In this season of body positivity and empowerment, if tucking in your shirt gives you life, do it.

trying to cover, tuck, and hide, what would it look like to own your
space, own your body, and own your fashion mistakes? You are
human! Give yourself some grace, woman!

Step Two: Mindfulness

Once my self-compassion had helped me to calm down a little,
I gave myself permission to feel my feelings and identify what was
behind them.

I felt embarrassed *because* I couldn't hide my belly rolls and
   muffin top.[v]
I felt sad that my efforts to lose weight weren't working
   because I'd been trying so hard.
I felt angry that I'd let so much self-hate spew out of my
   mouth *because* I know my body and my health are gifts
   from God.

Once I recognized why I was feeling what I was feeling, I
leaned into stating some truths as a way to help me bounce back.
What's true:

I am fearfully and wonderfully made (Psalm 139:14). I am the
temple of God and the Spirit lives in me (1 Corinthians 3:16).
Before I was formed in my mother's womb, God knew me
(Psalm 139:13). God fashioned me with purpose (Psalm 57:2
NLT). I am chosen (John 15:16). God has a plan for me and my
thiggy thiccck thighs (Jeremiah 29:11). No matter if I stick to

---

v. A "muffin top" is the part of your belly that folds over pants that are too tight.
It is also known as "cup-caking," as your belly pops over your pants like a
cupcake.

my healthy lifestyle or binge on french fries, God still loves me (Romans 8:1). And when the Enemy tells me that I'm disgustingly worthless, I can tell him to kiss my big, brown butt.

Step Three: Gratitude

All that mindfulness and Scripture are great, but I knew that to make it stay rooted, I needed to balance those facts and feelings with gratitude. I wish I could say I am a naturally grateful person, but I'm not. I work at it. Part of my daily discipline is journaling, so the day after my pink-satin-top incident, I pulled out my journal and filled an entire page with a prayer of gratitude about my body.

- Thank You for my health.
- Thank You that I can hold a ninety-two second plank.
- Thank You that I can do twenty-six push-ups without stopping.
- Thank You that I can cycle eighteen miles in an hour.
- Thank You that my yoga practice is increasing my flexibility, both physically and mentally.
- Thank You that I sprinted in my HIIT class[vi] today for longer than I ever have before.

You get the point.

I made myself fill out the entire page because I wanted to really integrate this sense of gratitude into my life. I wanted to fight to find all the reasons that I'm grateful for the body God has given me.

Now, this is where the rubber meets the road. The question I ask myself when I'm wanting to change something—a character

---

vi. HIIT stands for High Intensity Interval Training, but I feel a better acronym is "Help! I'm Indefinitely Tired." I'll tell you if it catches on.

trait, a habit, a pattern—is, Am I interested or am I committed? Do I *want* to build resistance or am I simply *interested* in one day, possibly, maybe getting around to building resistance? If we want to change, it begins with training our brains.

THE NITTY-GRITTY

Principles

- Frustrations may seem inconsequential, but our responses to them create patterns in our brains.
- Grit is gettable.
- Mindfulness is being aware of what God's doing *now* and removes our attention and preoccupation with *later*.
- Give yourself permission to feel your feelings and identify what is behind them.
- To prevent and restrain negativity bias, we must intentionally search and highlight the positive things in our lives.

Paul's Wisdom

"Take captive every thought to make it obedient to Christ." (2 Corinthians 10:5)

Prayer

God, I come before You fully aware of how negatively I criticize myself. You call me a poem, a masterpiece (Ephesians 2:10 NLT), and I call myself not enough. You say I'm fearfully and wonderfully made (Psalm 139:14), and I call myself unworthy. I come against the negativity bias and need You to help me view myself differently. I don't want to destroy what You have built, so help me love myself and others the way You do.

Your Word says my body is a temple (1 Corinthians 6:19), so empower me to treat my body with honor and value. Let my words, my actions, my emotions, and my thoughts focus on the positive, and help me retrain my brain. I want to see myself the way You see me—with love, self-compassion, and kindness. I don't want to live by the world's standards of beauty, but Yours.

Thank You for my thighs and my eyes, my nose and my toes. In Jesus' name, amen.

chapter eight

COMPARISON
IS A THIEF

*When they measure themselves by themselves and compare
themselves with themselves, they are not wise.*

PAUL THE APOSTLE (2 CORINTHIANS 10:12)

I mentioned earlier that I'm a twin—a younger twin, born just one minute after my sister, Jasmine. But that wasn't how it was slated to go down. See, I was *supposed* to be born first. Not only was I positioned ahead of her in the birth canal, but when my mother opted for a cesarean section, I was labeled as Baby A. Just to reiterate, I was going to be born first.

But then something shifted. Literally.

During the C-section, the doctors saw that my embryonic sac had broken and I had shifted under my sister, so the doctor pulled my sister out first. As a solo birther (what I call people who didn't get the privilege of having a wombmate—get it?), you might not find this meaningful, but for years, I had to live with the consequences of *not* being the firstborn. Jasmine got the first chorus of "Happy Birthday" all to herself because, technically, she was older. I even referred to her as my *big* sister. And for years she opened presents *first* because she was the *first*born twin.

Don't get me wrong: even though I had to share a birthday, being a twin is incredibly awesome. Did we play tricks on people growing up? Absolutely. Did we switch classes in high school? Without a doubt. Did I break up with her high school boyfriend over the phone because our voices sound the same and I love practical jokes?[i] For sure. Did we swap clothes and makeup throughout our teens? Yes, we did.

Though to some we looked identical, our interests were always very different. Jasmine wanted a skateboard; I wanted to dance. Jasmine was varsity cheer captain; I was captain of the varsity soccer team. Jasmine majored in business; I majored in art. Jasmine went to law school (there is a legal right and wrong for everything) and I studied aesthetics in graduate school (everything is interpreted artistically and individualistically). Though we are diametrically opposite in many ways, Jasmine is more than my twin sister; she's my best friend.

But there is a shadow side of being a twin. The *New York Times* article "Bringing Up Two at Once" discusses research that shows there is a high level of competition between twins that begins at birth. Even as infants, twins are aware of developmental growth differences. "A three-year study of 150 sets of twins completed by

---

i. Don't worry, friend! Jasmine discovered my joke and reunited with her boyfriend, who is now her husband.

Dr. Eve Lazar for the National Institute of Mental Health offers some interesting insights into this." She attributes competition and loss of identity in part to being "in constant company with a mirror identity."[1] In short, there is always someone to whom you will be compared.

Whether intentional or not, achievement among twins is always under scrutiny. Who walked first? Who spoke first? Who got better grades? Who ran faster? Who got the award? Who won the medal? Who got the job? Who married first? Living in constant comparison can have damaging effects on the psyche and value of self.

You might not have been born a twin, but in our current day and age, social media has created endless mirror identities. Every time you open a social media app, there are a million ways to compare yourself. Someone graduated college when you needed an extra year. They started a company while you're still trying to get your business model on track. They've started a family while you aren't anywhere near settling down, and on and on. Social media creates a constant means of scrutinizing both *success* and *self* that, left unchecked, can develop into anger and jealousy—anger that you are *not* and jealousy that they *are*.

Twinning

Consider the biblical twins Jacob and Esau. We find their story in Genesis 25, and it gives us some insight into what comparison and jealousy can create. Bear with me as I attempt to abbreviate their tale—welcome to the BIV (Bianca International Version).

> During ancient times—and even in some countries today—birth order was incredibly important. Not only did it determine the distribution of land and wealth, but birth order also determined a person's spiritual blessing.

Born to Isaac and Rebekah, fraternal twins Jacob and Esau were in conflict since the womb. Scripture even tells us that as the firstborn, Esau, was entering the world, Jacob held on to his foot like a gangster! Can you believe it? Lil Jacob was like, "Nope, you aren't gonna beat me! I'm coming with you." Even though Jacob was delivered *literally* on Esau's heels, it was Esau who was born first and thus received the birthright—everything from a double inheritance to land distribution, familial responsibility, and the authority of decision-making would be given to him, the firstborn son.

Scripture tells us Esau was not only the favorite of their father, Isaac, but he was also the alpha male who loved hunting and was also extremely hairy.[ii] After a long day in the field, Esau was ravenous and begged his indoor-prone, foodie-chef and mama's-boy brother, Jacob, for a bowl of stew. Jacob may have loved the indoor life, but he was savage. He offered a bowl of his bean soup in exchange for Esau's birthright![iii]

This really comes into play when their dad, Isaac, was about to die. Sure, you can judge Esau for making the dumb decision to give up his birthright for a bowl of stew. But as we are about to read, Esau wasn't stupid. Esau was following his father's desires. He was doing the right thing. He was obeying his father.

---

ii. How hairy do you have to be to get called out in the Holy Bible? Bless his heart.
iii. How good does your soup have to be to receive an entire inheritance? I'm asking for a friend.

Let's take up their story two chapters later:

"I am an old man now," Isaac said, "and I don't know when I may die. Take your bow and a quiver full of arrows, and go out into the open country to hunt some wild game for me. Prepare my favorite dish, and bring it here for me to eat. Then I will pronounce the blessing that belongs to you, my firstborn son, before I die." (Genesis 27:2–4 NLT)

As was the custom, a Hebrew father would lay his hand on the head of his eldest son and bless him before he died. This effectively granted the birthright-son status as the new head of the household. So here was Isaac—old, going blind, and about to kick the bucket. He called for his son Esau and asked him to prepare a delicious meal before he'd receive his blessing. In a final act of obedience to his father, Esau left to hunt for his father's last meal.

But in the shadiest of mom moves *evah*, Rebekah told Jacob to pull off the most epic twin prank of all time. She wanted to deceive Isaac into blessing her favorite son, Jacob.

She said to her son Jacob, "Listen. I overheard your father say to Esau, 'Bring me some wild game and prepare me a delicious meal. Then I will bless you in the LORD's presence before I die.' Now, my son, listen to me. Do exactly as I tell you. Go out to the flocks, and bring me two fine young goats. I'll use them to prepare your father's favorite dish. Then take the food to your father so he can eat it and bless you before he dies." (vv. 6–10 NLT)

Just one problem: Esau was hairy, and Jacob was not. What did Rebekah do? She devised a plan and covered Jacob with the skin of a goat.[iv]

Once the stew was made, Jacob went to his dying father's tent to serve him his last meal. To convince his father that he was Esau, Jacob lied repeatedly. Isaac was still unsure—remember, his vision had gone, but he recognized the voice as Jacob's. He called his son over for a kiss.

Jacob went over and kissed him, and when Isaac caught the smell of his clothes (sneaky mama Rebekah had dressed Jacob in some of Esau's finest 'fits), Isaac was finally convinced. "Ah! The smell of my son is like the smell of the outdoors," he said, "which the LORD has blessed!" (v. 27 NLT). Then Isaac proceeded to bestow the birthright blessing on sneaky Jacob.

> From the dew of heaven
> and the richness of the earth,
> may God always give you abundant harvests of grain
> and bountiful new wine.
> May many nations become your servants,
> and may they bow down to you.
> May you be the master over your brothers,
> and may your mother's sons bow down to you.
> All who curse you will be cursed,
> and all who bless you will be blessed. (vv. 28–29 NLT)

When Esau returned and found out his brother had stolen his blessing, a family brawl resulted like no other! Isaac discovered

---

iv. Can we depart from the Bible for one second to address this question yet again: How hairy was Esau and why didn't anyone help him manscape? But I digress.

he had been hoodwinked and began to violently shake. Although Isaac knew it was too late, Esau begged his father for a blessing. But Jacob had stolen it. The response from Esau's lips chokes me up every time I read it. It's a feeling I can deeply resonate with.

"Esau pleaded, 'But do you have only *one* blessing? Oh my father, bless me, *too*!' Then Esau broke down and wept" (v. 38 NLT).

Esau had done exactly what his father asked of him, yet he was met with a feeling of having been robbed.

What Am I Doing Wrong?

Have you ever thought, *I'm doing everything I should be doing but not getting what I thought I would get?*

I told my husband I was doing Whole30, a thirty-day program comprised of no sugar, no wheat, no dairy, and no fun. I invited him to join, but he said he didn't want to do it. After seeing all my meals and dedication to this plan, he joined me on day twenty and still cheated here and there. He said he did Whole30; I said it was more like Whole10. At the end of thirty days of stringent dieting and clean eating, I lost five pounds. But get this: Matt hopped on the scale and lost twelve pounds. Let that sink in: the man lost twelve pounds in ten days. There is nothing worse than doing what you're supposed to do and not getting what you thought you should get.

As trivial as that story might seem to you, it's wrapped in years of wrestling with weight, eating right, working out, and not getting the results I thought I would. I found myself saying, "I'm doing everything right, so why is everything so wrong?"

Maybe you have been trying to get pregnant with the man you

have been married to for years. And all of a sudden, your friend who's been shacking up with her boyfriend gets knocked up after 2.5 seconds. You're left wondering, *What did I do wrong?*

Maybe you've been single, sexy, and sanctified for years, abstaining from sexual activity because you want to do relationships the biblical way. You've been waiting for *the one*, the Boaz to your Ruth, when some hot young thing rolls into church wearing little more than a ball of yarn and sits next to *your* man.[v] You are praising the Lord with one hand and texting your friend with the other, saying, "I love Jesus, but I will *cut* somebody."

Maybe you've been doing the *most* at work. You're the first to arrive and last to leave. Your projects are pristine and always in ahead of deadline. Your output is solid, your attitude is the best, and they *still* hired someone else for the promotion you wanted.

You know what I'm talking about. If you haven't already, you will at some point feel like you are doing everything God asks you to do, when someone else swoops in and snatches up your blessing.

I get it.

When I was twenty-six years old, I was pinching pennies while I was in graduate school.[vi] I served weekly in youth ministry and volunteered at my church. I was single and desperately wanted to be in a relationship, but I could not get a date to save my life. In addition to living at home because I couldn't afford my own place, I was helping to care for my mom through stage 3 brain cancer. It was an incredibly hard season.

During this time, my twin sister got engaged to the most

---

v. I mean, he doesn't know he's your man yet, but he's your man. You claimed him.

vi. In full confession, I had a full-ride scholarship for school. I was pinching pennies because I had a convertible BMW I shouldn't have bought, so I was cleaning offices at night to try to earn extra income. Bless my heart.

perfect man in the world whom she'd been dating for six years—with a three-carat diamond. Please hear me: I absolutely *love* my sister. I was over the moon for her. But if I'm honest, deep down in my heart, I was really sad for me too. I felt deep longing and loss at the same time. I longed for what she had and felt enormous loss as my sister was leaving our birth bond to bond with someone else.

My situation wasn't exactly like Esau's—Jasmine didn't steal from me—but I did still feel robbed. When I compared my life to everyone else's, it didn't make sense to me. My friends—who didn't even love or serve God—were living amazing lives. I, on the other hand, was alone, living at home, and abysmally single.[vii] It felt like everyone was getting married, moving out, moving on, getting pregnant, getting promotions, buying homes, becoming bosses, and I had been forgotten. All the good and all the blessing and all the favor were given to everyone else but me.

There have been moments when I've struggled to hold the tension of happiness and sadness. In the struggle, I've probably looked as fake as a so-called designer purse bought out of the trunk of a car in a seedy alleyway.

"A new home? How amazing!"
"Another vacation? That's great!"
"A promotion? Good for you!"

My pearly whites were on full shine while inside I was breaking, wondering, *Why not me? When is it my turn?*

---

vii. If you are happily single, rock on. As someone born in a unit, there was a part of me that longed for a mate. But in no way does my longing for a partner mean I'm not a fan of happy and fulfilling singleness.

But when we focus on what we lack and compare that to someone else's blessing, it's never going to end well for us.

How to Break Free from Comparison

So how do we get beyond comparison? To find out, let's take a look at how Esau handled things.

Most people probably don't know what happened to Esau after Jacob stole his blessing. But let me bring in some history that might help us all get free from the bondage of comparison.

After Esau cried out to his father for a blessing, this is what he received:

Finally, his father, Isaac, said to him,

> "You will live away from the richness of the earth,
> and away from the dew of the heaven above.
> You will live by your sword,
> and you will serve your brother.
> But when you decide to break free,
> you will shake his yoke from your neck."
> (Genesis 27:39–40 NLT)

On first glance, this seems like a weak blessing, but reread that last sentence: "When you decide to break free, you will shake his yoke from your neck." Esau had an out! He eventually would be able to shake Jacob's control over him. But there was a requirement baked into the blessing. Did you catch it? Isaac told Esau that he had to *decide* to break free. In the same way, I want you to break free from the yoke of comparison. And if you want to break free, you have to make a conscious choice.

> If you want to break free, you have to make a conscious choice.

Decide

Are you ready to stop comparing? If comparison isn't gone, it's because you aren't ready. If every time they post on social media you cringe, you might not be ready to shake free. If every time their name is mentioned you involuntarily roll your eyes, you're still stuck in the bondage of comparison. If every time they advance you sigh, then you ain't ready to let it go, but you've got to.

The moment you let that comparison go, it has to let go of you! The yoke is broken.

When you decide what someone else has isn't going to hold
    you captive . . .
When you decide jealousy will not dissuade you . . .
When you decide comparison will not discourage you . . .
When you decide to break free . . .
. . . then you will shake off the yoke and *break freaking free*.

We usually don't hear about Esau in Sunday school or in sermons, but we most definitely hear about the exploits of his twin brother, Jacob. We hear about Jacob wrestling with God for a blessing. We hear about Jacob's name change from *deceiver* to *prince of many* (Israel).

But what happened to Esau? After the blessing debacle and subsequent brawl, Rebekah told Jacob he'd better skip town. She knew Esau was livid, and given the chance, he could've killed Jacob with his own two hands. If we ended the story there, we might scratch our heads and say, "Wow, Esau got the short end of the stick. He did everything his father asked him to do and still didn't get the blessing that was his birthright. Of *course* he'd compare his blessings to Jacob's. It was all so unfair."

If we aren't careful, we can feel that same way about our lives. The script we write internally sounds something like: I've been going to church faithfully, giving, tithing, leading, and serving. Why did someone else get what was supposed to go to me? Why did she get the promotion? Why did they have the baby? Why did they get the house? Why did she get the guy?

The list goes on, and you are right there crying with Esau. But that is not the end of his story. And it isn't the end of yours either.

Acknowledge Your Blessings

In Genesis 33, we see a great reunion between the twins. The last time we saw the brothers together, Esau was about to kill Jacob, but in this chapter, the two are reunited. Jacob was understandably leery about how Esau would receive him after everything that had gone down. So he devised a plan. He sent his servants, children, and wives ahead of him (with plenty of gifts too). Jacob sent livestock and beasts of burden that, if appraised in today's terms, would have had a value of almost a million dollars. Jacob hoped this would soften Esau's heart and, ultimately, spare Jacob's life.

When they were finally face-to-face, Esau was backed by four hundred soldiers. It seems safe to assume that Jacob was terrified, knowing vengeance and retribution would've been his just deserts.

He had deceived both his father and brother and was now being confronted by a massive army. In Genesis 33:3, we read that Jacob fell to the ground in a position of humility and bowed seven times before Esau and his army.

If Esau had chosen to settle the score, his army could've destroyed Jacob's entire tribe, taken all the spoils of victory, and then killed his brother on the spot. But Genesis 33:4 shows us an unbelievably gracious and countercultural ending: "Then Esau ran to meet him and embraced him, threw his arms around his neck, and kissed him. And they both wept" (NLT).

Wait a minute! Esau ran to his brother and embraced him? Esau hugged and kissed this man? Esau wept alongside Jacob in a joyous reunion? That doesn't sound like someone who is trapped in comparison at all! That doesn't sound like someone who is bitter or harboring resentment. When you can embrace what has hurt you, it's a good indication that its yoke is no longer your burden.

Here's the truth: you *decide* the yoke is too heavy and then *acknowledge* all that God has given you.

I could've been bitter and angry when my sister and all my friends were getting married. When everyone was working amazing jobs and getting promoted, I could've chosen to quit ministry. When those around me were buying new houses while I was living at home with my parents, I could've left the church and been angry with God. But to shake that yoke of comparison and break free of my discouragement, I knew I had to hold on to the knowledge that I, too, was blessed. I decided to stop looking at other people—even my twin—and decide daily to walk in the blessings of my own life.

Every day I would thank God in my journal and document what I was grateful for:

I have a roof over my head.
I have a job to pay the bills.
I have an amazing family, whom I dearly love.
I am succeeding in graduate school.
I am serving at my local church.
My mom has a remission diagnosis and is starting to live
  cancer-free.
I have started a blog that is reaching people online.
I have great friends who are committed to praying for me.

Years later, this discipline of acknowledging my blessings is still something I practice every single day. My life has changed so much, but the temptation to compare remains ever present. It's easy to get swept up in the success of *him*, or the body of *her*, or the church growth of *them*, so gratitude is my calibration. Even when life feels heavy or I feel like I'm not where I should be, I really fight for contentment. And when I say "fight," I really mean fight. I battle to maintain focus on the good I have already, even as I know there's still more I want from life.

I live in a house that I rent because I can't afford to buy it. But
  I'm choosing contentment and declaring I'm blessed because
  my home is beautiful, and I have a place to live.
I'm frustrated with my weight despite eating well and
  exercising daily. But I'm choosing to say I'm blessed to be
  able to have access to healthy food and the physical ability
  to move with ease.
I don't have any children of my own. But I am blessed to have two
  stepchildren whom I've helped raise since they were babies.

I don't have an easy or perfect marriage. But I'm blessed to be married to a man who is equally committed to making our marriage a picture of the gospel.

You may not have everything you want, but can you celebrate what you do have and strive to feel content? It starts with shifting your focus.

If comparison is the yoke that is choking you out, what would it look like if you bought maternity clothes for your friend who got pregnant while you're still waiting? What if you sent flowers to the coworker who got that promotion? What if you bought an awesome housewarming gift for your friend who just bought her summer home? Celebration breeds contentment. We get to decide that we are blessed and shake off the yoke of comparison.

If you keep reading in Genesis 33, when Jacob offered Esau all the amazing gifts, his brother said, "My brother, I have plenty. . . . Keep what you have for yourself" (v. 9 NLT).

Enough is a powerful word. Comparison is killed when we decide that what we have is enough. Sure, receiving more is a blessing, but enough is exactly that: enough.

I'm taking a little liberty here (yes, it's my disclaimer), but clearly Esau had done some internal work before reuniting with Jacob. His high-level grace was not the behavior of a man who was harboring bitterness, jealousy, or comparison. All those years later, Esau was living in the blessing of his father: "When you decide to break free, you will shake his

> **Comparison is killed when we decide that what we have is enough.**

yoke from your neck" (27:40 NLT). Did Esau shake it off? Baby, that yoke done been shooketh.

This is a powerful lesson for us today: you are not cursed just because someone else is blessed! When Esau walked in and saw his brother steal his birthright, he immediately thought he was completely out of luck. But big blessings for someone else doesn't mean there are fewer blessings for you. It's not pie!

Loose the lie that hangs around your neck. Their blessing doesn't equal *your* curse. In fact, it actually means God is in the neighborhood!

Step into Your Role

I get it. There are times when we feel as desperate and angry as Esau did. What we thought was promised to us feels like it has been taken. But don't forget your identity. You are a child of God. There will be times when big challenges make it hard to believe or trust that God loves you and wants you to be blessed. And if we aren't careful, we can become spiritual versions of Winnie-the-Pooh's friend Eeyore: blue, depressed, and pessimistic. *Things will never get better. I will never be chosen. I will never be blessed.*

Though Esau had a hearty cry in Genesis 27, his story didn't end there. He decided to break free of his yoke and step into his God-given identity. And Jacob was so moved by his brother's kindness that he saw the very face of God in him. And even as Esau said he didn't need gifts, Jacob continued to insist until Esau finally accepted them. With true reconciliation, the twins headed to their hometown as friends.

But there is an important detail in the narrative I don't want us to miss. In Genesis 33:12, Esau said, "Well . . . let's be going. I will lead the way" (NLT). Did you catch it? Esau not only welcomed the brother who had stolen so much, but he stepped back into his birthright role and led his little brother back home.

Wrestle

If you aren't where you feel like you should be—or maybe where you want to be—have you paused to think through why? Maybe it's just not your season. Or maybe you lack some important element—experience, education, or even age—and that's what you need to gain before advancing into what you're after. Unless we give an honest evaluation, it could be that our pride is blinding us to the reasons for where we are in life.

But let me shoot it straight. If God wanted you to be where you think you should be, you would've already been there. When we are in total alignment with what God wants of us, if we're honest and obedient, and there is still nothing we can identify to explain our circumstances, *that* is when we need to radically *trust* in Him. I don't know why God withholds people, places, or things from us, but I *do* know that His ways are greater than ours (Isaiah 55:8–9). If we don't have it, that doesn't mean we won't get it. It's just not now.

If you're familiar with the story of Jacob, you may have already heard this. But if you're new to the tale of these twins, check out this moment from the period of time after Jacob stole the birthright but before he returned home. Scripture documents in Genesis 32 that Jacob *wrestled* with someone (theologians believe this was God). He wrestled all through the night, refusing to give up until he was blessed.

I'm going to state and defend, based on the actions of Esau, that he, too, proverbially wrestled with God at some point before meeting up with his brother all those years after Jacob had robbed him. The man we see crying and begging in Genesis 27 is not the man we see blessed in Genesis 33. Esau knew how his mother felt about him. Esau heard what his father said about him. Esau saw how his brother was a conniver and yet blessed. Esau knew he was to be cursed until he broke free.

So I'm saying there had to be a defining moment, an inciting incident, something major that had shifted and caused Esau to change. There is no direct scripture to back this up, but we can clearly see the fruit of this decision. Esau had to believe in his blessing.

I believe Esau had his own come-to-Jesus moment long before he reunited with his brother, Jacob. That's why when Jacob came back home, Esau was able to stand in authority and confidence and mind-blowing forgiveness. He didn't need validation from someone else to tell him what he already was.

He was blessed.

Look Inward

In order to break out, we must look in. Too many times we are looking at external solutions to internal issues. We find ourselves saying:

If I'd only had a mentor, I would be doing better in my career.
If I'd just had more encouragement and affirmation, I would've succeeded.
If I were only _____ [insert married or a mom or single or younger], things would all be working out by now.
If I wasn't surrounded by all this negativity, I could achieve so much more.

But consider again the story of Esau. Just about everything he heard was negative. His mom said she liked his brother more. His brother basically said—even as Esau was going faint with hunger—"Bowl for your birthright, sucker!" His dad said, "You will live by your sword [have to fight for everything], and you will serve your brother" (27:40 NLT). Does that sound like a positive word was ever spoken over him?

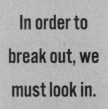

In order to break out, we must look in.

We have very little control over what goes on outside us, so to find solutions, we must look inward. Are you complaining that no one is doing anything to bless you? Are you blaming someone for doing something *to* you and using it as an excuse to never look within? Perhaps it's your own heart that needs a critical assessment, but you don't have to do it alone. Look at the way King David cried out to the Lord in Psalm 139:23–24: "Search me, God, and know my heart; test me and know my anxious thoughts. See if there is any offensive way in me, and lead me in the way everlasting."

If we are stuck in comparison, judgment, bitterness, or pride, we owe it to ourselves to ask God to reveal where we are harboring sin in our hearts. If we don't, those thought patterns will become a yoke around our necks. And removing this yoke is imperative—it's often so much heavier than we realize. We can try to convince ourselves otherwise: *I'm just a little bit jealous. I'm just a little bit bitter. The comparison isn't that big of a deal.* But God's Word is clear: if you don't break the yoke, the yoke will break you.

Left unchecked, the burdens of pride, bitterness, comparison, and judgment will turn into the language of resentment and defeat. And whether or not you realize it, these words will reflect your heart.

Why am I not blessed like them? I'm doing everything right.
I don't want to be in a small group anymore.
I don't want to serve at church anymore.
I don't want to go to church anymore.

Stop being choked by the yoke!

Decision

Once that heart search is completed, the next thing that needs to change is your decision.

If you're single and the yoke of comparison is making you feel less-than, choose a new *emotion*. (*I'm choosing to feel wanted and desired, even in my singleness.*)

If you're frustrated in your marriage because it doesn't look as good as someone else's, choose a new *declaration*. (*I'm declaring that I will work on speaking life over my marriage and choose to love my partner every day.*)

If you believe you will always struggle with health because everyone in your family does, *decide* to change the pattern. (*I'm going to treat my body like a temple and love it into health and wholeness with good decisions.*)

If you're stuck in a negative cycle of repeating the same mistakes over and over, intentionally *assess* what needs to change. (*I'm challenging my patterns and rote decisions to seek the newness that God can create in my life.*)

We need to look in, in order to break out.

When you decide, you will shake free.

THE NITTY-GRITTY

Principles

- Every time you open a social media app, there are a million ways to compare yourself.
- Social media creates a constant means of scrutinizing both *success* and *self* that, left unchecked, can develop into anger and jealousy—anger that you are *not* and jealousy that they *are*.
- If you want to break free, you have to make a conscious choice.
- Comparison is killed when we decide that what we have is enough.
- If God wanted you to be where you think you should be, you would've already been there.
- In order to break out, we must look in. Too many times we are looking at external solutions to internal issues.

Paul's Wisdom

"When they measure themselves by themselves and compare themselves with themselves, they are not wise." (2 Corinthians 10:12)

Prayer

Lord, help me not to fall into the comparison trap. To compare is to despair. My focus is on You, and I trust that You are doing something in me. Help me not to look to the left or the right but instead to focus on the race set before me. When someone else is blessed, help me celebrate them. When someone else gets what I want, help me rejoice with them. Guard my heart from bitterness, and remove the yoke of jealousy from around my neck. In Jesus' name, amen.

*For more on contentment, check out "Thankfulness, Gratitude, and Contentment" in the appendix, where I share the secrets to rewiring your brain, the power of gratitude, and expressing thanks.

chapter nine

DEPLETED, DEPRESSED, AND DISILLUSIONED

*So keep up your courage, men, for I have faith in God
that it will happen just as he told me. Nevertheless,
we must run aground on some island.*

PAUL THE APOSTLE (ACTS 27:25–26)

During the time that our church didn't have a permanent building—remember the U-Haul and that weekly load in and load out at the event center we rented?—I rolled into the parking lot at sunrise, prepared to begin the Sunday setup. The rickety building needed more than a new paint job; it needed a massive overhaul. The plumbing was a mess, and the bathrooms perpetually smelled like urine and dirty diapers.

One Sunday, hand to heaven, we came into the building to discover that an entire toilet was missing from the men's bathroom. Yes, an entire toilet. We were left to find a way to cover the hole in the ground and pray that no innocent child would fall into the abyss of poor plumbing, never to be seen again.

But this was our venue, and it was the right size for our growing church (read: it was all we could afford).

We arrived in our newly graffitied church trucks (a welcome-to-the-neighborhood gift, I suppose) and were surprised to see a crew from the prior night's events still working. We knew other groups rented the building on Saturdays, but rarely did events continue through the wee hours of the morning. Our crew was loading in while theirs was rolling out. It was certainly unusual, but I didn't really give it much thought.

I walked down the corridor into the main auditorium and saw empty alcohol bottles littering every corner. There was a long, wet, red-colored streak stretching the length of the main hallway. Before I could even determine whether it was actually blood (gag), our amazing crew of volunteers put on their gloves and started to scrub.

By the time I made it to the door of the greenroom, one of the volunteers asked me to wait outside so he could finish the cleanup before we started our production meeting. A few minutes later, I heard a yelp from inside. I rushed into the room and saw the volunteer holding up what looked like some kind of dead animal. "What is this?" he asked, disgusted. That's when I burst into hysterical laughter. It wasn't a dead animal, it was a discarded weave! An ugly, filthy, matted weave. Somehow it had found its way off someone's head and into the space between the couch cushions, only to be discovered by a young man who apparently didn't know a thing about fake hair. I wish the morning had stayed that funny.

Together, we finished cleaning the room and finally got everything in order. I was on my way to the dumpster with the last load of garbage when something on the stage caught my eye. I slowly walked toward it. There were little shiny spots almost everywhere, and I was concerned someone could slip on whatever it was as they were setting up for worship.

Suddenly the pieces came together.

I remembered seeing a poster in the venue of an all-male exotic dance group that was hosting a tour in the building.[i] And that's when I realized what was shining on the floor: body oil. Just hours before our morning service, half-naked men dripping with body oil were on the same stage I was about to use to preach the gospel.

I immediately went to the cleaning supplies and grabbed bleach and rags and whatever I could find to remove the remnants of slicky sin left on stage.[ii] I dropped onto my hands and knees to start cleaning and let my hair fall over my face to cover my tears. I wasn't crying at the fact that I had to clean (my husband might disagree). I was crying because no matter how hard we tried, our church couldn't seem to catch a break.

We were praying.
We were fasting.
We were tithing.
We were teaching.
We were believing.

---

i. Unfortunately, the visual of this poster is seared into the recesses of my mind, never to be forgotten. Barf. Purge my eyes, Lord!

ii. If you're wondering whether Clorox bleach cleans sin, it doesn't. But I didn't have the blood of the Lamb, so bleach had to do.

Yet we were still meeting in a disgustingly dirty venue full of blood-stained hallways, endless litter, ratchet weaves, and missing toilets! And now we were picking up after *strippers*?

At the end of the services—after the teardown team had packed up the equipment—I sat in my car alone, engulfed by the first silence I'd experienced since six o'clock that morning. In a parallel universe, I might have thought it was funny. I might chuckle and think, *How hilarious and wildly improbable.* But it wasn't another world; it was my real life. And in that moment, I wanted to drive away and never come back. No more setup, no more teardown, no more cleaning, no more church. I just wanted to quit.

Storms of Life

My father always warned me of the three big Ds of life: depletion, depression, and disillusionment. The truth is that it's hard to take new ground and move forward when you are *depleted*. It's painful to get back up when you are *depressed*. And it's challenging to maintain hope when you are *disillusioned*.

I get it. (Do I sound like a broken record yet?) I've been there. And so has our boy, the apostle Paul. Our quest for resilience benefits endlessly from the wisdom of this suffering saint. In fact, there is no other theology on suffering more profound than what comes from the pen of Paul. Through storms, both literal and figurative, Paul maintained his conviction even when wind and waves threatened to take him out.

You know that feeling that you are in a raging storm and there is no end in sight? When you feel stuck in a dangerous situation and don't think you'll make it out? If anyone gets it, it's Paul. In a storm that nearly took his life, he had a divine encounter that determined the destiny of everyone around him (Acts 27). I want to be like Paul and remind you that there is a plan, there is a mission, there is a destination, and we aren't going to die. If God gave us a promise,[iii] this isn't our end.

In the words of Paul, "I have faith in God that it will happen just as he told me" (Acts 27:25).

It was gutsy for Paul to profess this kind of faith *in the middle of a literal storm*. Ironically, Paul had already warned the crew not to head back out to sea, but there they were, *in the middle of a storm*.

Have you been in a situation that you didn't cause, but you had to clean up? Isn't that the worst? You didn't do anything wrong, but you're left picking up the pieces. It can happen to any of us, and we often don't know the reasons why.

This is hard for me. I like to have a reason! I was always the *why* kid.

Bianca, do your chores. *Why?*
Bianca, you need to obey. *Why?*
Bianca, take a shower. *Why?*

And since childhood, it's only gotten worse! I practically need a full spreadsheet to understand the reason behind certain situations.

As an adult, I'm *still* asking God the *why* questions.

Why did my friend betray me?
Why did my friend get sick?
Why did our plan fail?

---

iii. And to be clear, God has given us plenty. I put fifteen of my favorite verses in the appendix if you need a reminder.

What I love to see from Paul during this storm is the way he held the tension of both confusion and conviction as he conversed with the crew.

Confusion: If you would've listened to me, this wouldn't have happened.
Conviction: But because of my God, we *will* get to our destination anyway.

What we don't see at this moment is the *why*. Why did this storm happen in the first place? That's difficult for those of us who want to know a reason.

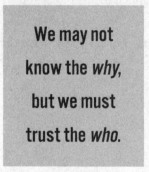

We may not know the *why*, but we must trust the *who*.

On the day I now affectionately refer to as Stripper Sunday, I wanted to understand a reason for everything that was going on. But even more, I needed reassurance that all this struggle was part of a plan, that all the pain would have a purpose. I can't say I ever got a satisfying explanation as to why some Sundays I was barricading toilet pits and others I was mopping up sweat and body oil. Unfortunately, friends, we don't always learn *why*. We may not know the *why*, but we must trust the *who*.

Why Versus Who

You might feel like this is a cop-out solution, but stay with me. When we linger in the *why*, we risk becoming bitter. When we focus on the *who*, we effectively surrender. And surrender is what leads us to meaningful encounters with God.

Let's jump back to the story of Paul. In the middle of a life-threatening storm, he was visited by an angel (Acts 27:23–24). What do we see here? Even in the scariest of moments, we are still positioned to encounter God.

I wish I could tell you that an angel appeared in my car on Stripper Sunday and told me that everything would work out in the end. Unfortunately, that did not happen. I couldn't even muster something wise to pray. I just simply showed up the next Sunday. And the next Sunday. And the next Sunday.

I didn't know why anything was happening the way it was. In fact, I still don't know why. I don't know why God would allow a homeless man to come into our volunteer break room and steal people's purses and wallets. I don't know why our iPads and speakers were stolen from our kids' check-in center at church. I don't know why our moving trucks were broken into—three times. I don't know the why, but I know the who. I believe God is good, and I believe God does good. I believe God has called me to serve the church, and I believe God will maintain the church. I know I won't always get a why, but I believe I can always trust the who.

And please understand: I know this is not easy. Trusting God is scary! But we can't put our faith in fear. We must put our faith in our Father who loves us. Ugh, I'm cringing even writing that sentence because it sounds so Pinterest-y. Just slap it on a watercolor floral arrangement and frame it in plastic rainbows, right? But, really, stick with me. Let's use Paul's situation as a model.

In Acts 28, we discover that Paul and the entire crew survived the treacherous night at sea and made it safely to shore, even though their boat didn't. (RIP ancient boat!) They hadn't, however, reached their intended destination. Instead, they ended up on an island called Malta.

Oh, someone give me a white hanky and a tambourine because I'm going to start a praise party. Why? Because the word *Malta* means "refuge." The comedic nature of God slays me! Paul survived a storm and ended up on Refuge Island.[iv]

But keep in mind, Paul had never been to Malta. He survived the shipwreck and dog-paddled to the nearest shore. And it turned out the shore belonged to a tiny island, where Paul, exhausted, realized he did not even speak the language.

Instead of arriving in Rome, where Paul had been headed to face trial before Caesar (arguably the most powerful man in the world), he ended up in Malta—itty-bitty little Malta.

Have *you* ever been to Malta? Not the island, silly. A proverbial Malta. Has there ever been a place that you thought you were headed, but you ended up somewhere entirely foreign instead?

What is Malta?

Malta is the divorce you didn't see coming.

Malta is the layoff you thought you could avoid.

Malta is the relationship issues you can't resolve.

Malta is the diagnosis that came when you felt completely
 healthy.

Malta is the bankruptcy that crept up on your business.

---

iv. If this was a modern rendition, I imagine it like the reality TV show *Bachelor in Paradise*. Think about it! Paul is single, but it's more like *Biblical Bachelor*, where you work really hard and almost die, but God comes through, and Paul wins a trip to Rome. Let's call the show *Refuge Island.* More details to come.

> Malta is the unexpected challenge you couldn't have dreamed
> was coming, until suddenly you were stranded in the
> middle of it.

I mentioned earlier that after the shenanigans of Stripper Sunday, I simply kept showing up and serving our church. What I didn't mention is that I was running myself ragged. We had no paid staff except our worship leaders, and I was still working two other jobs (that required extensive travel) to keep us in the black. I certainly wasn't overexerting myself for kicks and giggles, but I had a team to pay, commitments to honor, and a church to help fund. I was running on empty—absolutely depleted.

I began to feel waves of depression creep in (usually on Mondays after church), coupled with a punishing sense of inadequacy.

I should be a better leader to our team.
I feel like I'm constantly making mistakes.
We won't hit our budget at this rate.
No matter how much I study, my sermons aren't good enough.

Depression wasn't chemical for me; it was situational. I felt empty and unable to see the forest for the trees. I couldn't think of any way forward but to take a cue from Paul and just refuse to die at sea. In the words of the famous fish Dory, "Just keep swimming!" I swam until I found my Malta.

Paul made it to Malta—a refuge—but his time there wasn't easy. He was greeted warmly by the locals, who started a fire to warm him and the other survivors. And courteous guest that he was, Paul decided to help. But in the true *telenovela* fashion that only the Bible could document, Paul was bitten by a viper that was nestled in his armload of firewood and driven out by the heat of the flames (Acts 28:3).

Okay, okay. This is where I start shouting, "Nah-uh, bro. This [clap] ain't [clap] happening [clap]. God, give this man a break! He was already imprisoned and put on a ship he knew was doomed. He survived a storm, washed up on a foreign island—in the freezing-cold rain, mind you—and just when he was trying to be helpful to the natives, there was suddenly a venomous snake trying to take him out?"

There is a Yiddish proverb I learned while traveling in Israel that is said during trying times to lift your spirits. With shoulders raised in a shrug, you say, "But it could be worse!" Well, for Paul the Apostle, things just got worse.

It's in moments like these when the snake of disillusionment bites me. This is when I look at a string of disasters and—as a catastrophizer—I swear the end is near. I'm disillusioned and start reciting a mental list of all my flimsy reasons to give up hope:

1. I didn't hear from God.
2. There must be some sin in my life, and I'm paying the consequence.
3. I'm not good enough.
4. I want to burn the whole thing down and walk away.
5. If God loves me, why won't He intervene?
6. It's not supposed to be this way.

Disillusionment is feeling disappointed in the discovery that someone or something isn't as good as you thought it was. As I sat in the silence of my car after packing up on Stripper Sunday, I realized a painful truth: I was not only disillusioned with myself but I was also disillusioned with God.

Shake It Off

In moments of despair, depression, and disillusionment, we need to take a cue from our brother Paul and shake it off.[v] Literally, Paul shook the snake off and didn't suffer any effects from what should have been a lethal bite.

Friend, I'm gonna tell on myself and keep it real here: I am horrible at shaking things off and choosing to believe the best. But I want to emphasize that shaking off disillusionment is key to getting back up when life knocks us down. And when we shake that trash off us, we need not suffer any ill effects from it either. Meaning, when you start spiraling into disillusionment, you have to first stop repeating the lie that you've been abandoned by God and shake it off. But we have to take things a step further and make sure the venom of catastrophizing isn't lingering inside us.

Paul learned what we have to learn too: when we make it through the storm and all hell breaks loose on the shore—when we've been through it all and it still keeps coming—we've got to make like Paul and *shake! it! off!*

Pound your chest right now and say, "Get off me!"

Nah, you didn't do it. You didn't say it out loud. You said it in your head, and that doesn't count. Say it out loud so you can hear

---

v. I'm *not* saying you should brush off depression or ignore depletion. These are warning signs that we are not well. Always seek professional help when needed.

yourself make the declaration. Say it again so you feel it in your soul. Say it a third time so the devil and his demons start shaking!

The Bible gives us no record of Paul screaming, running around, or freaking out. Why? I think it's because he didn't do any of that. Paul knew he wasn't going to die on Malta. Paul didn't make a scene because he knew Rome was waiting, and Rome was where Paul would proclaim the gospel of the risen Messiah before Caesar himself.

Well, friend, I'm with Paul. I'm not going to die on *my* Malta, because *my* Rome is waiting too. Paul told his crew in the middle of a storm, "This has to happen." And I'm telling myself, "This *has* to happen" too. The vision God gave Matt and me for our church wasn't ours. It was God's. If God told us to build a church, then it *had* to happen.

If you've been on Malta trying to figure out why you're there, I want to point you back to the who. Who is in control of your life? Who loves you? Who gave you the vision or dream for your life? If you answered "God" to any of those questions, stand firm in the faith that has brought you this far. It's time to shake off the disillusionment.

This action isn't just for you. It's for everyone who is watching you too! See, when Paul got bitten by the snake, no one came around him to help. Everyone stood there and watched to see what he would do or what would happen.

> **Look at you! You are surviving and refusing to give up.**

Child of God, people are watching you. People are waiting for you to lose it, to walk away, or to curl up and die. But look at you! You are surviving and refusing to give up. I'm standing and giving God some praise because you're still here and you are going to shake it off.

Pick yourself up and get ready because Rome is waiting.

What to Do in Malta

Do we know what to do in Malta? If we find ourselves there, how should we live? Remember, dear friend, Paul didn't *want* to go to Malta either. Visiting Malta was not at all in his plan. And yet . . .

> You are living back at home with your parents and waiting tables when you *thought* you were on the fast track to a promising career after earning your MBA.
>
> You are going through painful IVF treatments after years of infertility when you *thought* it would be easy to get pregnant.
>
> You are moving out of the home you can no longer afford because you *thought* you would have been promoted by now.
>
> You are devastated because you *thought* your engagement would lead to marriage, not a broken heart.
>
> You're on Malta too.

Paul could've ended up bitten and bitter, but instead he made his time on Malta matter.

Word spread about the man who had survived both a storm and a snakebite, and Paul became quite popular on the island. He was invited to stay at the house of Publius, Malta's chief official. Paul was a bedraggled, foreign inmate who, before long, was invited to chill with the most prominent family on the entire island.

What if our adversity turns out to be the one thing that opens doors to which we otherwise would never have had access? Said differently, what if our adversity brings us opportunity? I think it would change our language. We would go from lamenting and asking *why, why, why?* to speaking, instead, with authority and clarity. Paul *had* to go through the storm, he *had* to survive a snakebite, because God was going to use him for something he never would have encountered otherwise. Sometimes opportunity is hidden behind adversity.

And that's not all. God had a whole bonus plan at play during Paul's months in Malta. Publius's father happened to be on his deathbed. While Paul was staying at the family's residence, he was perfectly positioned to perform a miracle. At what point did Paul realize he was in Malta for ministry? At what point did Paul awaken to the idea that maybe, just *maybe*, there were some miracles in Malta that had to take place? I don't know. But when a man who needs a miracle meets a man on a mission, get ready for some ministry to take place!

> Sometimes opportunity is hidden behind adversity.

Acts 28:8 says, "[Publius's] father was sick in bed, suffering from fever and dysentery. Paul went in to see him and, after prayer, placed his hands on him and healed him." Do you see what I see?

Scripture says Paul placed his *hands* on Publius's papa. I'm telling you that the hand that had been bitten by a snake was the same hand that was placed on Publius's daddy's head to bring healing. I don't think I'm reading too much into the text when I say: God will use the places we've been hurt to bring blessing to others who need healing.

I don't know what proverbial snake might've been dangling off your wrist last week, but you better start praising God for it right now! Why? Because what you went through didn't kill you. What you went through will bring other people confidence in *who* got you through it, even when they don't know the *why*.

What storm are you surviving?

I'm here to tell you that you're on Malta for a reason!

After Paul healed the dying man, word got around Malta. People from all over the island showed up at Publius's palace, which was transformed into a place of ministry and healing.

Paul wouldn't have known what was in store for him on Malta, but what he did know was this: it had to happen. In the same way, everything we have gone through and everything we will go through has to happen. It's part of the plan. And we believe the pain will have a purpose.

So until we make it to Rome, I want us to use our snakebitten hands to bring some healing to those around us. We may not know the *why*, but we're believing in the *who*. We can't quit in the storm because there is healing on the shore. It has to happen.

Years after Stripper Sunday, I still show up to our church Sunday after Sunday. Thankfully, we no longer meet in a busted-up venue that requires hours of arduous setup and teardown. The Lord brought us to a beautiful, permanent spot. Looking back, though, I'm truly grateful not just for the memories but for the ministry that took place in our Malta season that proved to me we didn't need calm waters to see God move. Despite our storms, people came to know Jesus in the most beautiful ways.

I'm not foolish. I know there will be more storms in my future.

That's just life, isn't it? I might find myself in despair, riding waves of depression, and even fighting disillusionment again. But now I'm tempered by the words of Paul, declaring that all that happens in my life has to happen. I'm reminding myself it's part of the plan. I won't quit because just as Paul finally made it to Rome, I know I will eventually end up where the Lord wants me. And guess what? You will too.

THE NITTY-GRITTY

Principles

- The truth is that it's hard to take new ground and move forward when you are *depleted*. It's painful to get back up when you're *depressed*. And it's challenging to maintain hope when you are *disillusioned*.
- We may not know the *why*, but we must trust the *who*.
- Disillusionment is feeling disappointed in the discovery that someone or something isn't as good as you thought it was.
- Shaking off disillusionment is key to getting back up when life knocks us down.
- Sometimes opportunity is hidden behind adversity.
- God will use the places we've been hurt to bring blessing to others who need healing.

Paul's Wisdom

"What is more, I consider everything a loss because of the surpassing worth of knowing Christ Jesus my Lord, for whose sake I have lost all things. I consider them garbage, that I may gain Christ." (Philippians 3:8)

Prayer

Lord, in moments of depression, disillusionment, or despair, help me focus on my who—You. I may not know what to do, but I'm trusting that wherever You have me, it's for a purpose. Wherever You have placed me, I'm declaring there is ministry to be done. Use the hurt and broken parts of my life to bring healing and hope to those who need it. Thank You for my Malta. In Jesus' name, amen.

chapter ten

WHAT TO DO IN
THE WAITING

*About midnight Paul and Silas were praying and singing
hymns to God, and the other prisoners were listening to them.*

ACTS 16:25

There was a time I felt utterly stuck. The sun rose with new and limitless opportunities, but as it set, everything felt the same. The day was new, but the issues were old. No matter how much positive thinking, Bible reading, verse quoting, and attitude changing I did, I felt imprisoned.

My desk was the same. My coworkers were the same. The feelings of hopelessness and frustration were the same. No matter how much money I saved, I still felt the pang of insurmountable debt. No matter how many lunches I prepared and packed—counting macros and calories—my weight stayed the same. No matter how many times I tried creating systems and structures for success, my workload felt heavier instead of lighter.

Have you ever felt stuck like that? No matter what you try, nothing seems to make much difference? This is the waiting period—the place where we linger until divine timing permits us to move forward. It might sound dramatic, but these seasons can feel like prison.

You are doing everything right. You are setting up a system for success. But you feel trapped in the system of *same*, a prison where nothing changes no matter your effort. But know this: grit and perseverance help us to develop more than the ability to wait. They help shape the way we *behave* while we're waiting.

> Grit and perseverance help us to develop more than the ability to wait. They help shape the way we *behave* while we're waiting.

And who might you guess would've understood that feeling? Paul, of course, our model of grit and resilience. He knew the feeling of being stuck in prison *because he was in prison*.

In Acts 16, we read that Paul and Silas were on their way to pray with their friends when a demon-possessed slave girl began to follow them. She was being used by her owners to tell fortunes in exchange for money, and she shrieked and yelled until Paul turned to her and cast the demon out. But once free from the spirit oppressing her (and telling fortunes through her), the girl was no longer a source of income to her owners. Needless to say, it didn't go over well with them.

Paul and Silas were taken to the local officials, stripped and beaten, then thrown into prison.

Just so we don't miss anything here, let's review some key points.

Paul was on his way to pray.

He was in community with other believers.

He delivered a girl from the shackles of demonic oppression.

And now he was being punished in prison.

With no release date set, Paul and Silas were chained and imprisoned like common criminals. But what did Paul do in the waiting? And how can that help us understand what we should we do in the waiting? We'll take a look at the story and see what tips we can discover through examining Paul's experience, but first, we have to get real about our current patterns of behavior.

Take a look at the list below and circle which choices are common during times you feel stuck:

Journaling

Listening to worship music

Calling a friend to pray with you

Serving others and investing relationally

Joining a community or church group

Exercising

Starting a new hobby

Finding a series on Netflix to lose yourself in

Eating your emotions and bingeing on snacks

Hopping on dating apps to distract yourself

Shopping excessively online

Spending hours on social media apps

Sleeping in, staying up late, or frequently napping

Do you notice a pattern? Are you proud of your choices? If you're anything like me, some of the behaviors you circled aren't exactly worth bragging about. I've squandered so much time with distractions and diversions that I've had to set up a new system to ensure I stay on track.

What to Do in the Waiting

Over the past ten years, I have discovered that if I don't intentionally set up rhythms for myself, I will easily end up returning to my old, unhealthy patterns. I'll sit and scroll endlessly, binge-watch *Real Housewives*, and eat my feelings to avoid having to actually feel them. To ensure I resist these temptations and stay motivated in my waiting seasons, there are five things I've learned from brain researchers to do consistently:

1. Work out (my body)
2. Get out (in nature)
3. Clean out (my space)
4. Go out (in solitude)
5. Sing out (like you can)

Don't get overwhelmed. I'm not adding more to your to-do list. I'm simply sharing the system I've created that works for me. You can copy it or create your own version to help you evaluate the most useful ways to invest your time during waiting seasons.

Work Out

Don't roll your eyes or throw this book at the wall. Trust me when I say working out is not only good for your body but it's also good for your brain.

When it comes to exercise, we know the usual benefits our doctors tell us at our annual physical. *Better sleep! More energy! Healthier heart! Go exercise!* But do you know that exercise helps us *wait*? Yes, physical activity is directly connected to the most important organ in our bodies: the brain.

Working out decreases feelings of anxiety. When you move your body, neurotransmitters like dopamine, serotonin, and acetylcholine are released into your brain. What does that mean? Well, physical activity releases these chemicals in our bodies and decreases feelings of anxiety and depression.[1]

Don't think you need seventy-five minutes and a gym membership to get this brain bump! Go on a fifteen-minute walk, take the stairs instead of the elevator, or put on music and shake what your mama gave you! There are no rules here. Just do something you love.

Working out improves your focus and concentration. In one of Suzuki's lab experiments, she found that just *one* workout can help improve the ability to shift and focus attention. Feeling blue? Confused? Stuck? Get up and move your booty. Not only will your focus change during a workout, but when you get your heart rate up, the positive effects of working out last for at least two hours after a half hour of exercise.[2]

With all the walking Paul the Apostle did, it's no wonder he had so many great conversations! You want a Damascus Road experience? Start moving!

Working out promotes the growth of new brain cells. One of the most powerful scientific benefits of exercise is that it "promotes neurogenesis, or the birth of new brain cells." "This is essential to improving cognitive function" as well as "the health and function of the synapses between neurons . . . allowing brain cells to better communicate."[3] In short, new brain cells mean new ways to pave new neuropathways.

Need a new way to think? Hop on a bike, go for a run, or simply stroll around the block.

Before you give all the excuses of why you can't possibly add hours of working out to your calendar, don't trip. If the idea of adding workouts to your already packed calendar feels daunting, start with doing half an hour of aerobic activity three times a week. If you can handle that, add ten more minutes to each workout. If you can handle that, add one more day. If you can handle that, well, friend, handle it because you are a boss. Job well done!

Consistency is key. Make sure to add this to your weekly routine, and before you know it, things that used to seem hard will have gotten easier and easier.

Get Out

Did your mother ever tell you to go play outside? Well, she was on to something. Growing up in a large family of seven, my mother knew the benefits of being outdoors. Not only is taking in nature restorative and grounding, but it's also calming.

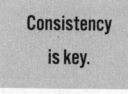

Consistency is key.

Now I confess, as a city girl, the idea of mosquitos, hiking, and campground toilets sounds like Dante's seventh circle of hell, but I recognize the power of being outdoors. Where we live and how we play has a massive effect on our health and mental well-being. New research indicates that being outdoors can reduce stress, fear, and anger, and even sharpen some of our cognitive abilities.[4]

Researchers, health-care professionals, and nagging moms all recognize the powerful impact environmental factors have on our mental health. Did you know that only 10 percent of good health is due to health-care services? Whereas an overwhelming 60 percent is linked to individual behavior and social and environmental factors.[5]

With this new science and research, medical professionals are now taking a look at how interacting with nature is affecting our brains. Let's take a look at what the really smart scientists say about fun in the sun!

The benefits of getting outside include:

- reduced stress and anger,
- increased feelings of kindness and generosity,
- reduced risk of developing psychiatric disorders,
- improved working memory, and
- improved short-term memory.[6]

So grab your sunblock, a hat, and a comfy pair of shoes, and spend a few minutes breathing fresh air, soaking in the sun, and getting out of your routine.

Clean Out

In a season of waiting—or as I like to say, a season of same—I need to find ways to keep my life moving forward, even if everything else feels stuck. One way to do that is to declutter and clean out areas that are causing emotional or visual chaos.

Did you know that clutter and visual chaos have a direct impact on mental health? Psychologists Repetti and Saxbe found that women who described their homes as cluttered or full of piles were more likely to be stressed and depressed than those who described their homes as organized and restorative. And if hormonal health is a concern for you, scientists and researchers are discovering that women with untidy or cluttered homes had higher levels of cortisol.[7]

To your beautiful brain, messy piles and clutter signal a lack of completion or pending projects. This can be highly stressful to your brain, *especially in a waiting season*. If clutter and unfinished projects in your home create stress and unneeded anxiety, then cleaning and organizing will empower you to take control of your home, improve your mood, and increase your focus.[i]

Control the environment. When life feels chaotic or unknown, cleaning can be a way to add some control to your life. Grab your mop and broom because cleaning can give you a sense of control over your environment. In fact, a study by the University of Connecticut found that in times of high stress, people default to repetitive behaviors like cleaning because it gives them a sense of control during chaotic times.[8]

If you find yourself wanting to scrub the tub or organize the bookshelf, that could be a sign that your mind is wanting to bring some organization—not just to your home but to your life.

Improve mood. Anxious? Don't worry about your manicure, and grab the dish soap, because activities such as washing dishes can help reduce your anxiety. A study published in the journal *Mindfulness* found that people who were mindful (remember this word from chapter 7?) when washing dishes—in other words, they took the time to smell the soap and to take in the experience— reported a 27 percent reduction in nervousness, along with a 25 percent improvement in "mental inspiration."[9]

---

i. What research is showing me is that between working out and cleaning out, my elusive six-pack of abs is just around the corner!

Increase focus. I'm neurotic about making my bed daily. Why? Researchers at the Princeton University Neuroscience Institute released a study that analyzed the effects of uncluttered and organized living. Paraphrased into non-neuroscience jargon, the study revealed that when your environment is cluttered, the chaos restricts your ability to focus.[10]

Did you catch that? Clutter limits your brain's ability to process information. Clutter is chaos, friend! When your room is a mess, you are prone to be distracted. Personally, I need to have at least one place in my room that is neat and tidy. Hence, my neatly made bed.

If you're feeling overwhelmed, take a long breath and calm your amygdala. You're fine. I'm with you.

Bianca's Sorting Strategy for Ditching the Clutter: *Love It, Like It, or Lump It*

1. Love It

   This pile is comprised of all the items you see yourself using or wearing within the next six to eight months. You may have an emotional connection to these items and see the immediate value of keeping the items in your closet, shelf, or cupboard.

2. Like It

   These are items (books, clothing, jewelry) that you have some connection to but could possibly give away or put in the garage. I'm a big advocate of giving items away. How do you know if you should give it away? If you think your sweater, lamp, or book could benefit someone else, then let it go!

> Like Shakespeare wrote, "Parting is such sweet sorrow," but a clean environment will make room for the new.
>
> 3. Lump It
>
>   I first heard this term in London while there for work, and I loved it. It's a simple way to express the need to get rid of something immediately (throw away, give away, or put away in storage). If you notice that your *lump it* pile is low or empty, it might indicate you have a hard time parting with items. Bring in a friend and allow them to help you decide what you love, what you like, and what you need to lump!

Go Out

This is going to sound weird to some of you, but trust me, it's amazing. When you feel stuck in a rut, in a season of waiting, or in a proverbial prison of despair, go out by yourself. Yup, you heard me. Go out! This isn't like the previously mentioned *get out*. *Get out* refers to spending time in nature, letting the sun hit you, and maybe even working up a sweat.

But going out is different. Going out requires you to spend time *on you* and *with you*. Yes, you heard me. This means actually washing your hair. This means shaving.[ii] This means putting on nice clothes. I am advocating going out *by yourself*. I've been a happily married woman for over a decade, but there are times when I need to go out by myself and get reacquainted with me.

Depending on your personality type, reserving a table for one might not feel easy or even like something you would want to do.

---

ii. Or not shaving if that feels like self-care. It's your life and your armpits.

But making time to sit alone, enjoy a nice dinner, and be still with your solo thoughts is a great way to listen to your own heart. In waiting seasons, we are prone to complain, lament, and ask for the season to change. I'm going to ask you to rewrite the narrative. I'm going to invite you to sit at a table with yourself and create space to hear from God. This might feel self-indulgent, but it's not. The practice will not only allow you to hear from God, but it will also create space to remind yourself of who you are, what you want, and what you are dreaming about.

> When you feel stuck in a rut, in a season of waiting, or in a proverbial prison of despair, go out by yourself.

When we go out with others—our colleagues, friends, or family—it's easy to let conversations linger around the surface. We want to catch up and chat about what's going on in the world, so we might worry about "bringing the mood down" if we discuss our problems, but that comes at the expense of connecting deeply on matters that are most important to us. When we go out alone, we have the opportunity to enjoy our own company as well as a chance to sort things out with the person who oftentimes gets in our way: ourselves.

Sing Out

Of all the listed waiting exercises, I saved this one for last because (a) it's my favorite, and (b) it's the easiest to do. You don't need hiking shoes, money, or extra time on your calendar. This can be done at any moment of the day because it simply means you lift your voice (tone-deaf or not) and "put a praise on it"!

You may or may not be familiar with that phrase, but I borrowed it from my sister-from-another-mister, Tasha Cobbs Leonard, from her song "Put a Praise on It." The lyrics are a constant reminder for me to keep praying, asking, and believing. In her words, not mine, I declare:

> There's a miracle in this room
> with my name on it
> There's a healing in this room
> And it's here for me
> There's a breakthrough in this room
> And it's got my name on it
> So I'm gonna put a praise on it[11]

When Paul found himself in prison, we don't see him angry with God or cursing the day he was born. In fact, we see quite the opposite. He worshiped the Lord with music while cuffed in a prison cell.

If *I* was thrown into the clink, the clanker, the slammer, or the joint,[iii] the last thing I would want to do is worship. In fact, I would most likely wind up in a ball on the floor of the cell, crying out, "Why, God, why? I shouldn't be here!" But Brother Paul? He was so hot and holy that he was worshiping the Lord while shackled, even late in the night.

Acts 16:25 tells us that around midnight Paul and Silas were singing hymns. Don't gloss over these delicious details! Go into the theater of your mind and picture Paul and Silas—bloody, bruised, and beaten, yet *still* putting a praise on it.

---

iii. Thanks to my time ministering in prisons, I've got the jail terms down! These are all nicknames for places of incarceration.

When Paul was in prison, he praised the Lord. I want to copy him. I want *us* to copy him.

Yes, sing out from solitary! Praise in prison! Worship as your warfare! Why? Because praise brings freedom. Acts 16:26 tells us that as Paul was praising, a great earthquake hit, and the chains fell off every prisoner. Though we might not be living in physical prisons, I firmly believe that when we worship in the waiting, we will experience a different kind of freedom.[12]

I could argue that Paul would cosign on my above points, but I'll let Scripture back me up on this:

- **Work out.** Paul had to walk everywhere. He definitely got his thirty minutes of daily cardio in, and if you doubt it, just check out his missionary journeys throughout the book of Acts. He racked up his daily steps!
- **Get out.** In Romans 1:20, Paul referenced the formation of the world as evidence of God's power and divinity. Clearly Paul appreciated the beauty of the outdoors because it reflected the power of God.
- **Clean out.** Paul knew abundance and lack, empty and full. And the best part? He was content in all of it. Check out Philippians 4:11–12 to see how contentment was the key.
- **Go out.** Did you know that Paul spent three years alone in the desert? Talk about alone time in nature! Not only was his solo time healing but it was also revelational. For more on what he learned in that season, read Galatians 1:11–20.
- **Sing out.** As we just read, put a praise on it.

What Not to Do in the Waiting

We've discussed what to do in the waiting, but let me also include a quick note on what not to do during the waiting time.[iv]

Freak Out

When nothing moves and you feel stuck, don't freak out. When we panic, we aren't in the headspace to make good decisions for our lives. According to psychologist Luana Marques, president of the Anxiety and Depression Association of America, high emotion erodes our ability to make well-reasoned choices.[13]

And *hello*! Paul said, "Do not be anxious about anything, but in every situation, by prayer and petition, with thanksgiving, present your requests to God. And the peace of God, which transcends all understanding, will guard your hearts and your minds in Christ Jesus" (Philippians 4:6–7). Don't trip, potato chip! God's got this.

If you need practical and simple coping mechanisms, here are five steps to help you manage your anxiety using the 5-4-3-2-1 method:

- Notice 5 things you see (notice the details of a rug or painting in the room)
- Notice 4 things you feel (feel the texture of your pants, pet an animal)
- Notice 3 things you hear (a honk from traffic, the ticktock of the wall clock)

---

iv. Disclaimer: I may or may not have done all the things listed in this section (possibly simultaneously), so please learn from my mistakes and try not to make the same ones.

- Notice 2 things you smell (a certain perfume, a candle, or wafting aromas of food)
- Notice 1 thing you taste (candy, coffee, gum)[14]

The idea is that the 5-4-3-2-1 technique helps you shift your focus to what's currently happening around you instead of what's making you feel anxious.

Make Out

Listen, the urges are real. I get it. Married or single, there will be urges to satisfy carnal cravings for new experiences. Different! Fun! Especially in seasons of stagnancy. But not all desires are meant to be acted upon. When we feel trapped, human and animalistic desires drive us to make impulsive decisions. Don't let the waiting make you desperate or foolish.

When our boy Paul wrote to his friends in Corinth—a city known for the people's sexual appetite—he told them, "Do you not know that your bodies are temples of the Holy Spirit, who is in you, whom you have received from God? You are not your own" (1 Corinthians 6:19). Don't get yourself into a *situationship* or compromise a current relationship because you are desperate to get out of what you're in.

Check Out

In the waiting, you might be tempted to abandon your pursuits altogether. You may want to throw in the towel and forget all about whatever goal you haven't reached. But hang in there, friend. You've got this. In fact, Paul said it this way: "Be steadfast, immovable, always abounding in the work of the Lord" (1 Corinthians 15:58 ESV). Don't check out; wait it out.

You might be one day away from breakthrough. You might be one lap away from finishing. You might be one song away from the ground shaking and your shackles falling off. Don't give up now!

Binge on Takeout

This gets touchy. But we've gotta go there! When we feel stuck, we can be prone to eat our emotions and try to cope through food. Now hear me: food isn't innately bad (I might even call it evidence that God loves us and wants us to be happy). But when we use food as a pacifier to cope with, calm, or control our emotions, we've weaponized the gift of nourishment that God has given us.

Paul warned against this in his letter to his friends in Philippi. He said, "Their destiny is destruction, their god is their stomach, and their glory is in their shame. Their mind is set on earthly things" (Philippians 3:19). You are more than your appetite. Trying to fill your soul-hunger through your stomach will only leave you wanting more.

No one can fill you like Jesus. No food can satisfy you like the Bread of Life. Even Jesus said, "For life is more than food, and the body more than clothes" (Luke 12:23). When our decisions are being made by our stomachs, we deafen the voice of the Lord.

Don't freak out, make out, check out, or binge on takeout. The waiting place is the perfect place to praise God. In fact, let's start right here and now by praising God for where He has us.

THE NITTY-GRITTY

Principles

- Grit and perseverance help us to develop more than the ability to wait. They help shape the way we *behave* while we're in the waiting.
- Consistency is key.
- When life feels chaotic or unknown, cleaning can be a way to add some control to your life.
- When you feel stuck in a rut, in a season of waiting, or in a proverbial prison of despair, go out by yourself.
- Don't freak out, make out, check out, or binge on takeout.

Paul's Wisdom

"Join together in following my example, brothers and sisters, and just as you have us as a model, keep your eyes on those who live as we do." (Philippians 3:17)

Prayer

God, I thank You for my waiting place. This pause in my life will not rob me of my worship. In the dark moments, in the quiet moments, in the moments when I feel trapped,

I will praise Your name and testify to the world that You aren't done with me yet. Help me not squander the moments of isolation, and let me see Your purpose even when it feels like I'm in a prison. In Jesus' name, amen.

chapter eleven

THE
DECLARATION
OF GRIT

Run in such a way as to get the prize.
PAUL THE APOSTLE (1 CORINTHIANS 9:24)

While on a trip with my husband in Boston, we did a walking tour of historical sites. It was interesting to see a replica of the Liberty Bell (rung at the reading of the Declaration of Independence in 1776) and consider how the sound of it had heralded the commencement of a new era.

Something about the ringing of that bell sparked my curiosity. As the United States' founders gathered in a room to put words around ideologies and thoughts, why couldn't I do the same for myself? *If others who have gone before me wrote declarations, what if I created my own declaration?*

Writing a declaration for your life isn't about positive thinking. It's about biblical optimism. In the book of Proverbs, Solomon told us, "As [a person] thinks in his heart, so is he" (23:7 NKJV). I knew I needed to create a philosophy for my declaration because my inner philosophy creates my thoughts. And as that famous saying goes, "Watch your thoughts, they become words; watch your words, they become actions; watch your actions, they become habits; watch your habits, they become character; watch your character, for it becomes your destiny."[1] So Solomon *was* right: as a person thinks in their heart, so they are.

> Writing a declaration for your life isn't about positive thinking. It's about biblical optimism.

Your declaration is a reminder of who you are, what you are called to, and who you're choosing to be. You are more than welcome to borrow mine, but I encourage you to write your own statement of what you are declaring over your life. Because I'm a Word nerd (read: Bible lover) at heart, I pepper in scriptures as the foundation to my statements. And of course, most of the verses are penned by Paul because, as I have shared, he is my favorite example of someone in the Bible who exhibited grit, endurance, and resilience.

I learned how to do this declaration exercise from communicators like Steven Furtick, Lysa TerKeurst, and Craig Groeschel, and now I love writing my own. Every year or so, I take time to write a new one to remind myself of what I'm called to in each changing season. You, too, might be inspired by their work, but don't shy away from writing something unique.

At the end of this section, I will walk you through an outline I developed to guide you in crafting your own declaration. Don't worry about making it pretty, perfect, or poetic. Write what your soul needs to hear, and it will ring as loudly as the Liberty Bell.

When I'm feeling like quitting or simply walking away, I go back to this declaration as a reminder of what I'm called to do in this particular season. It's not perfect or prolific, but it's mine. I'm sharing it with you as inspiration for what you will write next.

Enough

God, You are Jehovah Jireh—my provider.

You are the God who will provide my every need (Philippians 4:19) because You are the God who is more than enough.

When my soul is hungry, You are the Bread of Life (John 6:35).

When my soul is parched, You are Living Water (John 4:10).

You are my provider.

Since my mother's womb, Your hand of favor has been on my life (Psalm 139:13) and I'm declaring that *You* are my *enough*.

You clothe the lilies of the valley; You will clothe me too.

You feed the birds in the air; You will fill me with food.

You provide enough because You *are* enough.

I exist to prophetically proclaim Your Word to Your people.

You have fashioned me as a loyal people-developer, loving

truth-teller, and rebel revival-starter whose voice makes the Enemy cower.

So when words run thin, remind me that my tongue is the pen of a ready writer (Psalm 45:1).

Take my little and turn it into a lot.

You are my provider.

You are enough.

Serving people isn't something I do; being a servant is who I am (John 12:26).

I am anointed. I am creative. I am driven. I am loving. I am healed (Isaiah 53:5).

The world will know who You are through how I live my life.

I have enough and I am enough because *You* are enough.

Write Your Declaration

Now it's your turn! You can borrow from my declaration, but for this exercise to hold the most meaning, it's best when you articulate a visual or written declaration that is personal to you. Let's walk through this together so you can create your own.

Here is the flow I use to start writing a declaration:

1. Metaphor
2. Desires
3. Truths of Scripture
4. Commitment

Metaphor

What is a visual, an image, or a metaphor that resonates with you? For me, my high school hurdling debacle really framed my understanding of grit and resilience. Running was something I not only understood but had experience with. What might work for you? Here are some creative prompts to help get started:

- Life has felt like _____
  - a war (contentious, dangerous, intense)
  - a garden (seasonal, burdensome, unpredictable)
- My issue reminds me of _____
  - drowning (overwhelming, paralyzing)
  - flying (frightening, treacherous)
- This problem is as complex as _____(image)
  - a poem
  - a painting

Desires

Once you have an intention, theme, or metaphor for your declaration, begin to list out your desires. It might be a large social issue like fighting human trafficking or a more personal desire like breaking the stronghold of anxiety. For me, I had to remind myself that God is my provider and will always give me what I need. Once I identified my metaphor, I could craft words around my desires.

What are your desires? Here are some ideas of things you might consider:

- *I want to be strong because I feel weak.*
- *I want to be wise because I feel foolish.*

- *I want to increase confidence because I'm emotionally bankrupt.*
- *I want to develop self-control because my desires drive me.*
- *I want to walk in freedom because addiction controls me.*

Truths of Scripture

Now, this is my favorite part. When we feel like we don't have words to speak over our issues, or perhaps we don't have answers to our problems, the Word of God is full of promises and wisdom.

> When we feel like we don't have words to speak over our issues, or perhaps we don't have answers to our problems, the Word of God is full of promises and wisdom.

I love leveraging Google to help me find scripture for a particular situation. Simply google "Bible verses about _____ [enter your topic]." Then hit Search! You will be surprised at how many amazing scriptures are available for your declarations. Please understand: I'm not bending Scripture to fit a particular problem. What I am doing is letting God's Word remind me of His truth.

- Feeling alone? Check out Isaiah 41:10; Deuteronomy 31:8; Psalm 37:23–24.
- Feeling anxious? Check out Philippians 4:6–7; Jeremiah 29:11; Isaiah 40:31.
- Feeling depressed? Check out Exodus 14:14; Romans 8:28; Isaiah 40:29.

Commitment

And finally comes the time where we make our commitments. What are you vowing? What are you promising to do? What are you publicly committing to?

- I promise to remain faithful even when I feel faithless.
- I vow to not give up even when I am weary.
- I won't stop believing for breakthrough.

Spend some time with your journal or a blank digital document and create a declaration for whatever you are facing in this season. When you're happy with it, power through to the next section of this book. Well done, friend.

THE NITTY-GRITTY

Principles

- Writing a declaration for your life isn't about positive thinking. It's about biblical optimism.
- Your declaration is a reminder of who you are, what you are called to, and who you're choosing to be.
- When we feel like we don't have words to speak over our issues, or perhaps we don't have answers to our problems, the Word of God is full of promises and wisdom.
- To write a declaration, use metaphors, desires, truths of Scripture, and commitments.

Paul's Wisdom

"Do not conform to the pattern of this world, but be transformed by the renewing of your mind. Then you will be able to test and approve what God's will is—his good, pleasing and perfect will." (Romans 12:2)

Prayer

Jesus, You do not quit. On earth You endured every hardship and never failed in Your obedience to the Father.

You completed everything He asked of You. Thank You, Jesus, that You finished all that is necessary for salvation with Your death and resurrection. You endured what I could not. You are faithful and true. You start and You finish.

I confess that I'm in a season when I want to quit. Even with small and simple, I sometimes want to throw in the towel and walk away. Specifically, I confess that I do not want to continue and persevere in _____. Forgive me. I acknowledge my brokenness and weariness.

As I look at my lack and ineptitude, the challenges in my life, and the sufferings in the world, I admit some fear and anger. I fear that I won't make it or that I will fail horribly. I am creating scenarios in my head that are causing fear and anxiety. This is rooted in the pain of _____ that happened in my past. I'm currently worried _____ won't come through. If I'm honest, doubt sometimes swallows my faith in You. Please carry me through. Please help me make it.

I turn to You, the "God who gives endurance and encouragement" (Romans 15:5). I ask that I would be "strengthened with all power according to [Your] glorious might so that [I] may have great endurance and patience" (Colossians 1:11). Your Word says that "suffering produces endurance, and endurance produces character, and character produces hope" (Romans 5:3–4 esv). Give me strength to take the next step and the faith to believe that You will keep giving me grace and strength when I need it.

I rest in You, God, the strong one who does not quit on any of Your promises, including Your promise to never leave or forsake me.

In Jesus' name, amen.

PS: If you are feeling brave, I encourage you to post your declaration online and share it with your friends and family. It will help you be accountable and possibly inspire others to do the same. Tag me, @BiancaOlthoff, so I can see it too!

THE POWER OF STAYING: IT WILL ALL BE WORTH IT

chapter twelve

FIGHT THE
GOOD FIGHT

*I have fought the good fight, I have finished
the race, I have kept the faith.*
PAUL THE APOSTLE (2 TIMOTHY 4:7)

Ⅰn the fall of 2022, my family gathered at The Ark Montebello
to celebrate the thirtieth anniversary of the establishment of
this church in industrial East Los Angeles. We sat in the glow
of sunset peeking through the church windows as seats filled up
quickly. Electric energy filled the sanctuary auditorium, like the
track stadium in my high school glory days. Everyone was excited
to celebrate the many victories that had taken place over three decades. Years full of weddings and funerals, joy and sadness, all in one
building, all with one family.

The Juárez crew found seats in the front row and the band

walked onstage. When my father joined them there and welcomed everyone, the audience rose to its feet, cheering loudly. My dad, the man who had led this church as pastor faithfully and without compromise, humbly choked back tears. Everyone was cheering, and they weren't just cheering for *him*.

I would wager that if asked, not one person in that auditorium (or the packed overflow room in the adjacent building) would've said they were there to celebrate a *man*. Instead, everyone knew that the church had not been built by one man but by an entire body of believers who called the place *home*, a refuge of safety and security amid the concrete jungle of East LA. But we stood and honored a man who faithfully and consistently led the congregation for thirty years.

As various staff and congregants shared memories from their years at the church, I thought back over the myriad challenges through which my father had led them. Not just the internal stuff, like managing services and facilitating outreach, but major societal changes and acts of nature. He led the church through:

Civil unrest and the Los Angeles riots in 1992.
A massive earthquake that devastated Greater LA in 1994.
The fear of Y2K affecting financial structures in 2000.
National panic following the terrorist attacks on
    September 11, 2001.
My mother's brain cancer battle in 2006.
The economic recession and financial downfall of 2008.
A global pandemic in 2020.

Day by day, week by week, month by month, and year by year, my father pressed forward and led a growing congregation.

What began with fifteen people in a living room expanded into the thousands. The church is comprised of mostly urban blue-collar families, and the heart of the dedicated community impacted not only Los Angeles but the world. During his thirty years of leadership, my father was committed to creating a compelling vision to serve others. This led to:

> launching missionaries around the globe, from Romania to Japan;
>
> building a mission house and a subsequent shelter for battered children and women in Mexico;
>
> creating a food pantry at the church to feed the local community;
>
> hosting free concerts, conferences, and community events; and
>
> more than thirty thousand salvations.

In addition to these large-scale efforts, the church's weekly ministries helped single mothers find community, provided support to those battling addiction, met the needs of inner-city youth, and offered pastoral counseling to those who sought it.

I'm breathless just thinking about all these years of managing and expanding a growing ministry, but to my dad, it was like breathing. Serving was his oxygen. The day we celebrated thirty years of impact and service as a church, one might think it had been easy—or at the very least, it was done with ease. But as someone who grew up and watched her father serve selflessly, I saw the cost and the toll it took on him to get back up after life knocked him down.

None of it was easy, but some moments were positively painful.

I saw people abandon the church or speak negatively about my father, all the while knowing how my father had supported and helped them. I saw him weather storms of leadership, budget deficits, and building projects. I witnessed moments when my father gave of his life and wondered, *Is it worth it? You've been knocked down so many times, why get back up?*

Legacy

The definition of *legacy* for a Jesus follower is far deeper than money or property left in a will. The idea of *biblical legacy* includes our contribution to the next generation. Biblical legacy is an inheritance—it's your gift of service to others. It's also a gift you give yourself because it plays a part in your finding genuine fulfillment.

The core of biblical legacy is the belief that what you pour yourself into will have a lasting impact. The art you create, the children you raise, the business you build, the scientific contribution you make, the classrooms you affect, the debt-free living you commit to, or the music you compose—*this* will be your legacy, and it will influence future generations.

> The core of biblical legacy is the belief that what you pour yourself into will have a lasting impact.

With every step closer to your purpose, with every sacrifice endured, with every promise from God that you hold on to, with every trial you survive, you are adding to the foundation of faith for the next generation to stand upon. The ripple effect of your life will reach future generations—for good or for bad, whether you want it to or not. You are making a mark one way or another, so the question is, What mark will you leave?

While sitting at the church anniversary celebration, I flashed back to a moment when I'd seen my father fight in the midst of an ugly and undeserved struggle. I watched him persevere in the face of humiliation to push toward the legacy he was determined to leave.

It had been over two decades prior when my dad invited me, as his guest, to attend a conference where he'd been invited to speak. It was a very important event, and I was honored to be his teenage assistant for the day. There were six speakers, over a hundred staff, and thousands of guests in attendance. My dad led a main-stage session right before the lunch break. But instead of the usual hangry (yes, that's hungry + angry) conference attendees who normally fill the room ahead of mealtimes, the crowd was palpably electric. Dad preached unabashedly and made the Bible come alive. One moment the auditorium was in rapt silence and full attention, and the next they were roaring with laughter, on the verge of tears. The response to the gospel was overwhelming, and by the end of my dad's session, the entire auditorium stood in a rousing call to belt out the old hymn, "I Have Decided to Follow Jesus."

After this session, the guest speakers were taken to a room where a catered lunch was to be served on a long conference table. The table only had seats for the pastors, so I pulled up a chair near the wall. My father, a charismatic man with enough humor and charm to light up any room, humbly thanked the other speakers, who stood in ovation as he entered the room. There was no denying it: everyone loved my dad.

Well, everyone *but* the conference host.

The conference host had wheat-colored hair and light skin that had been wrinkled with age and leathered in the sun. His steel blue eyes hid behind hooded, heavy lids. A brutish man known for ruling with an iron fist, he loved keeping everyone in line. By any standard, he was tall, but with my father seated, the host towered over him.

While my father told a story and everyone laughed, the conference host sidled up behind him and started making fun. He sneered at my dad's outfit and mocked his shirt. He imitated my dad's Mexican accent in a disparaging tone. He critiqued my father's lack of formal education. He laughed at my dad's connection to the crowd, dismissing it as "entertainment."

Everyone went silent as the oxygen seemed to drain from the room. The host's jokes weren't funny; they were mean. The host started rubbing my father's back as if it had all been in good fun, but soon, his hands were high enough on my father's shoulders that it looked like there might be a strangling. The host's contact was so intense, I watched my dad swaying like a bobblehead toy. He endured the caustic and unrelenting jokes with pursed lips and a gentle smile. Without the satisfaction of whatever reaction he had been expecting, the host raised his hand behind my father's head as the room looked on in horror. *Is this a joke, or is this man going to hit my father?* I thought in disbelief. The host cocked his hand farther back, then dramatically and with a loud *thwap*, he slapped the back of my father's head. My dad's head flung forward from the blow. No one moved.

I can still see my father's dignity in that moment, even as his head hung low. Whether with shock or embarrassment or radical forgiveness, my dad gently shook his head from side to side and smiled as if it had all been a joke. But the room knew it wasn't a joke. And I knew my father wasn't going to retaliate. True to form and character, my father humbly smiled and did what he always does: he picked his head back up.

As I sat in The Ark Montebello auditorium twenty years after that incident and listened to my dad—head held high—I realized that his years of sacrifice weren't just for God, his family, or the community. His grit—even in the face of opposition—allowed us to experience freedom in Jesus and taught us how to persevere and pour ourselves out for others.

The Legacy of Paul

I'm adamant about redefining legacy because it isn't only left by the wealthy. Take a minute to think of a great leader. That leader has come to the forefront of your mind because he or she left a legacy. Nelson Mandela helped defeat apartheid and became South Africa's first Black president. Laurance Rockefeller conserved thousands of acres of park land. Marie Curie discovered radiation and was the first woman awarded a Nobel Prize. Albert Einstein changed our understanding of the entire universe. Mother Teresa loved so well she was canonized as a saint. These people understood that leaving a legacy is the way our lives can make lasting impact.[i]

Part of the problem with our culture's postmodern mood is a fascination with the present and an absolute self-absorption. *What's in it for me?* When we make decisions about our future, we

---

i. Not one of these leaders mentioned left a will for one person or an inheritance for a few. Their impact changed the lives of millions.

must remember our future will be different—more purposeful—when we think of others before ourselves. John said this about Jesus (John 3:16); Paul said this (Acts 20:35); and Peter said this too (John 6:68).

Asaph, the author of Psalm 78, also knew this and reminded us to declare the faithfulness of God to the next generation. In verse 4, he said, "We will not hide them from their children, but tell to the coming generation the glorious deeds of the LORD, and his might, and the wonders that he has done" (ESV). Legacy is shouting Psalm 145:4 to a deafened world and believing it is true: "One generation shall commend your works to another, and shall declare your mighty acts" (ESV). Often, we don't realize the weight of our decisions. We think our choices are isolated and independent. But they are so much more. Whether we want to admit it or not, our decisions could have lasting impact on generations to come.

Paul's life was marked by pain, loss, abuse, and abandonment. But one of the hallmarks of this gritty and resilient leader is that he didn't view his life as his own. His legacy was to live his life as an offering unto God. Paul was keenly aware of the time required and sacrifice necessary to create a legacy. He spoke about his life using several analogies in Scripture (2 Timothy 2:3–7), such as

a runner in a race—he was committed to the course;
a farmer planting seed—he was patient in waiting for the harvest;
a soldier in battle—he was willing to fight for freedom.

No matter our age, background, or ethnicity, we all understand these images and metaphors.

When Paul wrote to his friends in Philippi, he shared an

interesting analogy about his life. He said, "But even if I am being poured out like a drink offering on the sacrifice and service coming from your faith, I am glad and rejoice with all of you" (Philippians 2:17). Upon first reading, the idea of being poured out might feel wasteful or accidental. But for our brother Paul, it was all *intentional*. In the mindset of Paul, if his life *wasn't* being poured out, it would be wasteful. This verse comes from a letter Paul wrote from a prison in Rome. His crime? Preaching the gospel. His punishment? Potentially his life. His posture? Filled with joy and rejoicing for his friends.

In Genesis 35:14, when Jacob set up the pillar for worship at Bethel, he consecrated it by "pour[ing] out a drink offering on it." There was a similar ritual commanded in the Law. In Exodus 29:40–41, it says the priests were to offer a "drink offering" of a *hin* (Hebrew liquid measurement equal to about five and a half quarts) of wine along with the lamb of the burnt offering. They would pour the wine out as part of the sacrifice that was offered.

The visual image Paul painted for us in this verse is a poured-out drink offering. Some scholars suggest Paul was referencing the Old Testament act where wine would be poured out on a place of sacrifice (Exodus 29:40–41). But let's take a look at cultural context to see whether Paul was referring to something not just relevant to the Philippians but revelational to the church. Theologian A. T. Robertson suggests that since the Philippians were living in a pagan Greco-Roman culture, this phrase would have had other implications. The readers of Paul's letter knew of the pagan practice of pouring out wine from a glass as a sacrifice to a god. Rooted in ancient Greece, this act was done when people wanted to "pave a way" when seeking their god. As was their custom, they would pour a little bit of wine from their cup when they drank as a sacrificial gift to their god.[1]

Paul (ever-so-brilliantly) took a cultural practice the Philippians would have known and wrapped it in biblical truth. When Paul said, "I am being poured out like a drink offering," he meant his life was being poured out as a sacrifice to the one true God.

This was a continuous act of pouring out. His last drop of life wasn't poured out until he wrote his second letter to Timothy (his son in the faith). He wrote, "For I am already being poured out like a drink offering [that's the same Greek word as in Philippians], and the time for my departure is near. I have fought the good fight, I have finished the race, I have kept the faith" (2 Timothy 4:6–7). *Drip, drip, drop.* Paul gave everything he had! His life was a sacrifice poured out.

When we look at Paul's life holistically, we see that the sacrifice was a daily activity. He gave up what most people would boast in—his education, his pedigree, his social clout—and didn't stop there. Paul told the Philippians that his background, his religious heritage, and his accomplishments were counted as "loss." And he didn't stop there. He told his friends in Philippi, "What is more, I consider everything a loss because of the surpassing worth of knowing Christ Jesus my Lord, for whose sake I have lost all things. I consider them garbage, that I may gain Christ" (Philippians 3:8). Instead of leveraging his pedigree or boasting in education, Paul poured every last drop out for the gospel, for the church, and for the Lord. His life after meeting Jesus on the Damascus Road was a drink offering to the Lord.

Prior to dedicating his life to Christ, my father had his own

Damascus Road encounter, which opened his eyes to the life he was living. Addiction to drugs and alcohol and relationships with women attempted to cover guilt and shame. His constant drinking and party lifestyle were setting him up to repeat generational cycles, giving his life away for good times and bad repercussions. He was on track to repeat the generational cycle of alcoholism, abuse, and purposeless living like his father and his father's father. When my dad heard the gospel, he had no clue what that would mean for his life. But the idea of a relational God who loved him and could provide spiritual forgiveness captured his heart and changed his mind. Instead of running *away* from God, he ran *toward* God.

> Like Paul, my father had to face people who didn't understand or agree with his new way of living.
> Like Paul, my father was ostracized and marginalized from family and friends upon conversion.
> Like Paul, my father was viewed suspiciously by religious insiders who questioned his motives and commitment.
> Like Paul, my father cared passionately about explaining and proclaiming the gospel.

When I think about Paul's resilience and his absolute refusal to quit, I can't help but wonder:

> Did Paul know he would have an audience with influential political and religious leaders?
> Did Paul know he would train up the next generation of the church?
> Did Paul know he would perform miracles?

Did Paul know he would write letters that would be read for
more than two thousand years?
Did Paul know how his life and writings would shape the
church forever?

No. No, he didn't. Paul had no clue where the Lord was taking
him or what would be asked of him. But he continued to obey. His
footsteps paved a path for us to follow:

His incarceration teaches us how to worship while in our
proverbial prisons.
His confidence while confronting storms teaches us how to
believe we will find solid ground.
His refusal to let beatings stop him from preaching teaches us
to proclaim the gospel even when we are in pain.
His resilience and commitment to God teach us that freedom
awaits us *and others* if we don't give up.

How to Leave a Legacy: Follow Me

In his letter to the Philippians, Paul told his friends to practice what
they'd seen him do. This is a common encouragement from Paul,
who wrote to the Corinthians and told them the same thing: "Follow
my example, as I follow the example of Christ" (1 Corinthians 11:1).
If Paul was living his life as a sacrifice, if Paul was being poured out
for others, then he encouraged us to do the same.

When you were a kid and someone asked you what you wanted
to be when you grew up, I highly doubt you said you wanted to be

a poured-out drink offering. Not only is the metaphor odd, but you would also be odd for saying it. Who wants to give up their life to be poured out?

I'm sure Paul's friends and family thought Paul wasted his life by giving up power, prestige, and political influence. But Paul obeyed the call and served until there was nothing left. And I would safely wager that Paul probably questioned his choice to walk away from the life he once lived and the promise of a secure future. What was the benefit? What did Paul gain? There was no popularity, notoriety, or life of ease. But Paul obeyed because God asked.

You might be reading this and find yourself thinking, *I could never give myself away. I don't want to pour myself out. What a waste.* But let's be very clear: You *are* pouring out on something. You just might not know what it is.

Maybe you are pouring out your life on ambition and acceptance. Maybe you are pouring your life out to acquire finances, influence, and status. Maybe you are pouring out your life for the pursuit of happiness or the American dream.

And the truth is, when you pour out in the wrong places, it will leave you empty.

Your life can be poured out on *your* ambition, *your* desires, and *your* pleasures. Or your life can be poured on the people, places, and promises of God. Where will you choose to pour?

> When you pour out in the wrong places, it will leave you empty.

Nate Saint was the missionary pilot who has been quoted as saying, "People who do not know the Lord ask why in the world we waste our lives as missionaries. They forget that they too are expending their lives . . . and when the bubble has burst they will have nothing of eternal significance to show for the years they have wasted."[2]

I'm not saying cash out your retirement plan, sell your dog, and go on some gnarly mission trip. I'm not asking you to start a church, move into a jungle, or launch a ministry for orphans. I'm simply asking you to evaluate where you are investing your life and what you are giving yourself to.

> If you're a Pilates instructor who wants to create a space
>> where people can feel whole, do it.
> If you're a stay-at-home mom who wants to start a business,
>> do it.
> If you're an aspiring doctor who wants to serve the
>> underprivileged, do it.

You don't have to have all the answers or the perfect plan. My dad had no clue what starting a small Bible study in East Los Angeles would lead him to. He didn't know what would come of it. But he obeyed God, decided not to quit, and his life has affected thousands of people.

Lessons on Legacy

Legacy is something that is intentionally built. You must decide *now* what you want to leave for future generations. It won't be easy. It might not even be clear. But if you obey God and pour out your life where He wants you to, your impact will change not only your life but the lives of generations to come.

This can all feel overwhelming, but if our brother Paul says, "Follow my example" (1 Corinthians 11:1), then let's do just that! Using Paul's life as a model for legacy, let's pull out some practical principles on how we can build our future now.

> You must decide *now* what you want to leave for future generations.

Conviction

When you have a conviction about something—someone to connect with, a place to go, a role to step into—don't ignore it. The Holy Spirit could be prompting you with a holy hunch to pour yourself out in that area for a season. If there is a nudge or prompting, don't write it off.

We see in Acts 16 that Paul had a conviction to travel to Macedonia to preach the gospel. His sensitivity to the prompting of God led him to a whole new region where people were able to hear the truth of Jesus.

> During the night Paul had a vision of a man of Macedonia standing and begging him, "Come over to Macedonia and help us." After Paul had seen the vision, we got ready at once to leave for Macedonia, concluding that God had called us to preach the gospel to them. (vv. 9–10)

You might be saying to yourself, *Yeah, but Paul's conviction was backed up by an angel appearing to him.* I get it, and I've said the same thing too. But there are countless other times when Paul's decisions were based simply on the unrelenting pursuit of getting back up and completing what was asked of him. That's conviction!

Good Decisions

The decisions we make today affect our tomorrows. Paul's life was comprised of a string of decisions to obey God. From the moment he encountered God on the Damascus Road, Paul made the decision to obey. Constantly and repeatedly, we see Paul obeying the promptings and convictions of the Holy Spirit through the course of his ministry. And with history to prove it, the decisions Paul made daily affected the church indelibly.

There will always be circumstances out of our control, but our responsibility is to continue making good decisions despite that. Paul didn't choose to be beaten, shackled, and imprisoned in Philippi (Acts 16). But he *decided* to use the opportunity to worship and praise God. He *decided* to not abandon the jailer who was going to take his own life. And he *decided* to share the gospel with the jailer and his family, leading to a revival of faith in the entire city of Philippi!

No matter how difficult a situation, one thing we can always control is our response to it. Let's respond with good decisions.

Small Changes

It is easy to feel overwhelmed by a broad goal like "get in shape" or "give sacrificially." But if you know you need to incorporate exercise into your health routine, the reality is, working out even once a week for forty-five minutes will lead to almost fifty hours of workouts for the year. If you know you should be tithing to your local church, but 10 percent feels like too much of a jump, start with giving 1 percent. The hardest part of changing is starting. Start with a small change, knowing it can grow into something bigger.

Paul made a small decision to witness to the jailer who kept watch over him in Acts 16. When the earthquake broke the chains of every captive in the prison, Paul decided not to flee. Instead, he consoled the jailer who had been about to take his own life and led that man to Jesus. Paul led the jailer's whole family to Christ. One small decision in prison led to a whole revival. Amen!

Embrace Pain

Pain isn't only physical, and Paul experienced plenty of that during his ministry. We know he was stoned, starved, and snakebit—that was certainly hard on his body. We also know Paul suffered with a proverbial "thorn in [his] flesh," something he asked the Lord to remove three times (2 Corinthians 12:7–10). And as we see in 2 Timothy 4:10, Paul was also abandoned by Demas, his colleague in ministry. I'm sure that hurt a great deal too. But in the midst of all this, Paul kept forging ahead. He knew what was ahead of him was more important than who left him.

When creating a legacy, not everyone will understand or agree with all your decisions. In fact, your commitment to the future might even annoy or frustrate those who are living for the present. But legacy leaders are willing to embrace the pain, remain committed to their convictions, and know that little changes make a big impact. Therefore, the pain is worth it.

We experience all kinds of pain throughout our lives, but redeeming the pain in order to leave a strong legacy will require us to get up after we fall. We will fall, fail, and falter, not because we stink but because sometimes life does. We must always find ways to stand back up. Paul said it best:

> That is why we never give up. Though our bodies are dying, our spirits are being renewed every day. For our present troubles are small and won't last very long. Yet they produce for us a

glory that vastly outweighs them and will last forever! So we don't look at the troubles we can see now; rather, we fix our gaze on things that cannot be seen. For the things we see now will soon be gone, but the things we cannot see will last forever. (2 Corinthians 4:16–18 NLT)

Tell Others

Did you know that two-thirds of the New Testament books were penned by our boy Paul? There are so many people whose lives were changed and influenced by disciples, apostles, and followers of Jesus. But Paul did something that few others did: he told others what he learned and saw in culture and Christianity. Paul was intentional about penning truths and explaining the nature of God. Because he was committed to telling others about what God had taught him and had done in his life, we now have a greater understanding of who God is.

When we think about influencing the future, we need to ask who we are currently sharing our lives with. Who are we sharing our stories with? When we testify to the faithfulness of God—the job we received, the home we bought, the business that started—we bring others into celebrating the goodness of God. In almost every letter Paul wrote, he shared the pain and problems he endured. Not for sympathy or attention but to highlight that God met him and provided a way through. When we share our stories with others, it empowers them to do the same.

Sometimes God redeems stories by surrounding us with people who need to hear about our pasts in order to help protect their futures. Other times it's simply necessary to display our heartaches so someone else can have hope.

And Yet

On the night of the church's thirtieth anniversary, I thought about the people who'd abandoned my father, spoken ill of his vision, or even walked away from the Lord altogether. He'd spent years sowing seeds into the hearts of men, women, and children, and many times, he never saw the return. He had shed tears for loved ones who passed away while maintaining faith for healing.

And yet . . .

Through it all, my father would show up to a church he considered a second home. Faithfully, day after day, week after week, and year after year, he drove onto the campus with burdens on his heart but a smile on his face. No matter what was ahead of him that day, he made the daily decision to love, pray, teach, preach, and believe for those he led. For thirty years, my father planted seeds, not knowing when—or if—he would see a harvest.

Isn't that the unpredictable nature of agriculture? Do we know what seed will sprout? Do we know when fruit will grow? Do we—with certainty—know when harvest will happen?

I sat in the front row of the church where I grew up and listened as my father testified to every person watching, live and online, that God is faithful. Against all odds, though they had sailed straight into the wind, without enough money, God had sustained the church—not a building or a location but the people of God—for well over thirty years.

As a church planter for only a tenth of the time as my father, hearing his words felt like breath in my lungs. His stories were hope in a season of hopelessness. His church was a testament to the value of sacrifice, and the people who filled it were fruit of a life well lived.

When you tell others of where God has met you, provided for you, loved you, and enabled you to get back up, it teaches them to do the same.

THE NITTY-GRITTY

Principles

- The core of biblical legacy is the belief that what you pour yourself into will have a lasting impact.
- You must decide *now* what you want to leave for future generations.
- The decisions we make today affect our tomorrows.
- When you pour out in the wrong places, it will leave you empty.
- The hardest part of changing is starting. Start with a small change, knowing it can grow into something bigger.
- Legacy leaders are willing to embrace the pain, remain committed to their convictions, and know that little changes make a big impact.
- Sometimes God redeems stories by surrounding us with people who need to hear about our pasts in order to help protect their futures.

Paul's Wisdom

"Follow my example, as I follow the example of Christ." (1 Corinthians 11:1)

Prayer

God, when my efforts seem insignificant, remind me that small changes make lasting impact. Allow me to live today with tomorrow in mind. Let my time, talent, and treasure be used to expand Your kingdom here on earth. Let me live with legacy in mind and faith in heart. May my life be poured out like an offering to those around me. In Jesus' name, amen.

thirteen

IT'S JUST ME AND JESUS

*In all these things we are more than conquerors
through him who loved us.*

PAUL THE APOSTLE (ROMANS 8:37)

Well, friend, we did it. We made it to the end of our journey and completed this book. You are gritty. You are tenacious. You are resilient. You said you were going to finish the book, and you did. I'm high-fiving you, wherever you are, because we crossed the finish line together. Come here. No, come closer. Let's hug it out. I'm so proud of us!

You set out with a vision to read this book, and you conquered it. And to paraphrase our brother Paul the Apostle, you are more than a conqueror (Romans 8:37). If you don't necessarily *feel* like a conquering warrior today, it's okay! You know what I discovered?

When we are around people who feel like conquerors, it strengthens our faith because faith is contagious. So grab a comfy seat, and let's remind ourselves of what we are called to.

Some people are called into politics. Some people are called into the home. Others are called into ministry or medicine. Me? I'm called to bring freedom. Plain and simple, I was made to set the captives free through the transforming Word of God. This isn't a glorious calling or job that promises a lucrative future. Whether working in an anti–human trafficking organization, ministering in prisons, or preaching the gospel in churches, my calling is clear: bring freedom in Jesus' name.

But the results sometimes make me question my calling. When no one responds to a gospel message, am I doing what I'm supposed to do? When I pray for someone and their situation remains the same, did I really hear God's voice lead me on this path? When I preach a studied and passionate word but no one seems to receive it, did I make a mistake choosing this calling?

> No matter what confusion or lack of clarity you may be facing, don't stop forging ahead.

As children of the Most High King, our identity is clear. But sometimes our callings aren't. Your mission might feel cloudy. Maybe your life has shifted. Maybe you are finding new passion for your calling. No matter what confusion or lack of clarity you may be facing, don't stop forging ahead. Put one foot in front of the other, and repeat this daily.

In our journey through this book, we have spoken about resistance, depression, disillusionment, failure, feeling stuck, and feeling beaten up. I've told you this 439 times already, but I must say it again: there *will be* opposition. In this life, there will be moments when you want to quit, cower, and call it a day. You aren't alone. When Paul knew the Romans were dealing with similar issues, he encouraged them in the same way I'm encouraging you. Whether the opposition is physical, spiritual, financial, emotional, or relational, we are *more* than conquerors.

> A conqueror will never win if a conqueror never fights.

But note this: a conqueror will never win if a conqueror never fights. We have to be willing to get back up and fight our next fight, to wage war on the lies of the Enemy, and to step into our callings like we are stepping foot into our promised land.

More Than Conquerors

Now, if you are familiar with the Bible, you might know Romans is a no-nonsense book in which Paul lays out theology and Christology with such urgency you'd think he was late for a date. It's deep. It's profound. It's applicable. And sometimes it's hard to understand. But sandwiched in the middle of the letter is a lovely, straightforward section that reminds us of our identity as followers of Jesus.

In Romans 8, Paul told us that there is no condemnation in Christ Jesus (v. 1). We have been set free from the law. *Hallelujah!* Our minds have peace because of the Spirit of God. We are no longer slaves and serfs, but we are children and coheirs of the Most High God. Our present sufferings are nothing in comparison to the future that awaits us. And we know that all things work together for good for those who love Him (v. 28).

Paul—like a lawyer—laid out an airtight case to make sure we know that there is nothing that can come against us. Look at the progression Paul made in Romans 8:

> In verse 31, we see that opposition cannot separate us from God.
> In verse 33, we see that accusations (from someone who comes against us) cannot separate us from God.
> In verse 34, we see that condemnation (the belief that God is against us) cannot separate us from God.
> In verse 35, we see that no one can cause separation.

Now that we have that context, consider verse 37 again: "In all these things we are more than conquerors through him who loved us." This verse really sounds good in an Instagram post, crocheted on a pillow, or painted on a mug. But let's not miss out on the true power in what Paul was teaching.

Paul was writing to the Roman church, which was not only facing persecution and prosecution but was also oppressed in every way. In chapter 8, Paul reminded them—and us—of the power we possess as the people of God. We will need to be resilient; we will need grit; we will need to cultivate perseverance for this life. But we aren't doing this in our own strength. The power of the Spirit of God will give us what we need.

Romans 8:37 isn't a statement of probability or possibility. It's a statement of reality. How do I know this? Because in my own struggle to push past nerves, negative self-talk, and insecurity, the power of the Spirit of God has allowed me to pour myself out like a drink offering. Even in the midst of my inadequacies and insecurities, the gospel has gone ahead of me. I've repeatedly quoted the words of Paul in my mind: *I am more than a conqueror. I am more than a conqueror. I am more than a conqueror.*

Sometimes when I'm preaching this powerful truth at a conference or in a church, I feel a wave of insecurity wash over me. Out of nowhere, the nerves are back and I'm feeling dizzy. The dewy glow on my face is definitely now just sweat. I'm not preaching for the room—I'm preaching for *myself.*

The literal translation of Paul's phrase "more than conquerors" is "to go beyond a concise victory." The Greek word for this expression is *hypernikaō* (pronounced hoop-er-nik-AH-o).[1] By using the prefix *hyper-*, Paul was basically saying, "I'm trying to say *victory*, but *victory* isn't big enough, so what I really mean is that the love of God gives us glorious hypervictory."

There wasn't one Greek word to describe this power and victorious mindset, so Paul took two words and brought them together to attempt to describe "more than a conqueror." God's love and grace has empowered us to be hyperconquerors.

Hypervictory for Jesus

In March 2022, I had an opportunity to speak on Romans 8 at a conference in Dallas, Texas. I had such a weight on me as I prepared for this word. There was so much going on personally in my life that I just wanted to run away. But instead, I bought a bubble-gum-pink power suit, put on white high heels, backcombed my hair for extra, extra volume, and went to battle.

Thousands of eyes watched as I stepped onto the stage to

preach the Word live—and hundreds of thousands of eyes watched online from around the globe. With trembling hands holding my Bible, I turned to Romans 8:31–37:

> What, then, shall we say in response to these things? If God is for us, who can be against us? He who did not spare his own Son, but gave him up for us all—how will he not also, along with him, graciously give us all things? Who will bring any charge against those whom God has chosen? It is God who justifies. Who then is the one who condemns? No one. Christ Jesus who died—more than that, who was raised to life—is at the right hand of God and is also interceding for us. Who shall separate us from the love of Christ? Shall trouble or hardship or persecution or famine or nakedness or danger or sword? As it is written:
>   "For your sake we face death all day long;
>   we are considered as sheep to be slaughtered."
>   No, in all these things we are more than conquerors through him who loved us.

At this point in my Texas teaching, the excitement was high. I was feeling beads of sweat drip down my back because I was amped, and the Word of God made me want to spit fire. Why? Because Paul had done jumped out these pages, taken us by the collar like a drill sergeant in battle, and basically said, "Buck up, child of God. Life is tough, and so are you."

In my teaching, I revisited verse 31. But I didn't read it verbatim to my Dallas darlings and international audience. Nope. I added my flava and read it like I heard it in my head: "If God is for us, who in hell can be against us?"

I felt the room get tight-bootied and clutch their proverbial pearls. They appeared to be shocked at my word choice, but I was theologically correct. If the Enemy is Satan, who's been banished to hell, and if (like Isaiah 54:17 says) no weapon formed against us will prosper, then why were we acting shocked? The truth is, there is no person on earth and no demon in hell that can come against my God.

> There is no person on earth and no demon in hell that can come against my God.

My pink power suit and me went rogue. I stepped away from my notes and began to preach from my heart. In the middle of my own teaching, I, too, needed a reminder of the *Him* Paul was talking about. If we don't know the power of *Him*, we doubt the conqueror *in us*.

Let me talk about *Him*.

The God who spoke and time began . . .

The God who parted the sea from the land . . .

The God who called night out of day . . .

The God who causes mountains to quake and land to shake . . .

The God who lifts the sun and dips the moon . . .

The God who sees our heads hung low and lifts our gazes high . . .

The God who knows our past and still grants us a future . . .

The God who is over all and under nothing . . .

The God who leaves the ninety-nine and searches for us . . .

The God who promises us a future and a hope . . .

The God who will never leave us nor forsake us nor forget
us . . .
The God who loves us and forgives us . . .
The God who feels our pain and knows our shame . . .
The God who knows our fears and sees our tears . . .
The God who hung in shame and who rose from the grave
for our gain . . .
The God whose death brought us life and whose resurrection
brings us hope . . .
We are more than conquerors in Him . . . that's who.

I walked offstage and grabbed a tissue to wipe my face. Oh yeah, friends. I was *definitely* sweating. I grabbed my things and headed to the bathroom (read: I needed someplace private to dry off). In the long backstage corridor, production guys were running everywhere, and security guards checked access badges. I leaned up against the wall to catch my breath, whispering the only words I could muster in that moment: "Lord, sharing your Word can be hard. I feel alone, but I know You have called me to this. Remind me—even now—that I can be victorious because You are with me. Show me that You are with me, and may lives be changed by Your goodness."

As I lifted my head and continued toward the bathroom, I saw the back of a woman in the distance wearing the bright green volunteer shirt they gave everyone who served at the event. She turned around, and we caught eyes. Her chocolate skin and kind smile looked familiar, but because of the distance, I didn't recognize her. I was nearly in the ladies' room when I heard a voice yell, "Pastor Bianca!"

The volunteer in the bright green shirt was calling my name and waving at me to come toward her. If I'm being honest, I really didn't want to talk to anyone. I needed a moment to collect my thoughts. I was sweaty, exhausted, and truthfully, kinda in my feelings. I took a deep breath and before I could respond, she threw her hands in the air and shouted the hook I could never forget: "It's just me and Jesus! It's just me and Jesus!"[i]

A chill ran down my spine, and I stopped dead in my tracks. My mind flashed back to a sprained ankle and my determination to carry on. *No. No way. There's absolutely no way*, I thought as I stood frozen.

When the security guard asked whether I knew the volunteer, "Hell yeah, I do!"[ii] came instantly flying out of my mouth. "It's just me and Jesus!" I shouted back and ran over to find myself in the arms of Mia, the unforgettable queen I'd met in prison four years earlier.

Grit Don't Quit

I never thought I'd see Mia again. Yet four years later, there she was, in a completely different city and a completely different wardrobe. Long gone was the orange jumpsuit of incarceration, and this woman of God stood proudly, free from bondage, both literal and spiritual, more than a conqueror. I sobbed into her neck as we embraced like long-lost friends.

She explained that by the time she'd realized I'd be speaking at the conference, the event was already sold out. Not to be deterred, she signed up to be a volunteer, hoping we'd somehow be able to connect.

---

i. If this doesn't sound familiar, go back to chapter 6.
ii. That would've probably been considered the bad version of that word. I'm half hood, half holy. Sorry, Mom!

As the good Lord would have it, we did, and in a hallway in Dallas, Texas, we sang the hook to the greatest prison praise song I've ever heard: "It's just me and Jesus! It's just me and Jesus!"

Friend, you never know what your resilience will prepare you for. For me, resilience allowed me to preach the gospel to Mia and worship in prison. For Mia, resilience was not allowing her past to mark her future. She is more than a conqueror who is now sharing the gospel in her community. Your yes might bring freedom on the other side. Your grit might be the very thing that inspires others to get up and keep going.

You, my dear, are a gritty and resilient conqueror! Don't be afraid of your trials, trauma, and tribulations because resistance is a sign you are going in the right direction—and you never know how resilient you are until resilience is the only choice you have. But you do have to *choose*. You have to decide that you will use every challenge you face to make you stronger.

You are not alone. It's you and Jesus and an army of conquerors who will remind you that you can do this. And with every new hurdle you soar over, tell others it's possible.

Prayer

God, give us the grit we need to obey and follow You. Your Spirit has equipped us, and we can do all things in Christ. As we follow You and serve You, remind us that we are more than conquerors in You. Thank You for giving us purpose, calling, and divine empowerment for our lives. In Jesus' name, amen.

EXTRA READING FOR EXTRA CREDIT

Fight the good fight of the faith.
PAUL THE APOSTLE (1 TIMOTHY 6:12)

During high school, I started boxing at a local gym. I didn't start sparring (practicing with a partner in the ring) until college. The lessons I learned in the ring still ring true today. In fact, I learned the phrase *throw in the towel* from my boxing coach. The origin was first used in a literal sense, but now it is used metaphorically.

In the early 1900s, boxers moved from using sponges to towels to clean up blood and sweat from fighters. When a fighter was unable or unwilling to continue fighting his opponent, his coach would throw a towel in the middle of the ring to signal their fighter was finished. The saying began to be used figuratively in the early 1900s to mean to give up, to surrender, to concede defeat.[1]

There are a series of questions a trainer or coach will consider before pulling a fighter out of the ring. These same questions can serve us well as we evaluate whether or not to continue on. Questions like:

- Is the fighter just tired, or are they injured?
- Is the fighter still mentally capable of making critical decisions?
- Is the fighter topically wounded or internally bleeding?
- Is the fighter able to continue, or will there be irreparable damage done?

In the same way, we need to ask ourselves some questions during difficult seasons. With all this talk about perseverance and resilience, is there ever a legitimate reason or season to throw in the towel?

You might be frustrated with the discipline you've been
putting in without seeing results.
You might be frustrated with your job.
You might be frustrated with friendships.
You might be frustrated with your spouse.
You might be frustrated with all the above.

It can be surprising how much better your life can become if some adjustments are made. What if the issue you have with your work environment is the same problem management wants to fix?

What if your friend is just as frustrated with communication patterns as you are? What if your spouse wants the same shifts in love and respect that you do? If you quit now, you won't ever see what *could be*.

The truth of the matter is, if you walk away from your goals/ job/friend/spouse and go somewhere else, there are going to be issues there as well. No matter the season you step out of and into, you will face frustration. But like a wise mentor once told me, "Don't let temporary problems lead you to make permanent decisions."

Five Questions to Ask Before You Quit

Before you throw in the towel, I want you to ask yourself five critical questions to help you think strategically and not emotionally.

What *Exactly* Is Frustrating Me?

Pinpointing the issue is the first step toward solving it. We need to get specific here. We must identify the issue, or we will get stuck in our feelings. *I'm not feeling seen. I'm not feeling heard. I don't feel like I'm growing. I don't feel loved. I'm feeling exhausted. I'm feeling like I'm done.* We have to clearly identify the root issue.

Let me give you some prompts to help identify some possible reasons for frustrations:

I'm not feeling seen. → I don't feel like my work or efforts matter.
I'm not feeling heard. → I don't feel valued in this relationship.
I don't feel like I'm growing. → I don't have opportunities to expand.

I don't feel loved. → I have unmet needs.

I'm feeling exhausted. → I don't have good boundaries in
place.

I'm feeling like I'm done. → I don't have the emotional
capacity to make this work.

You need to clearly define what's frustrating you. If you don't
know the problem you're solving, then you're likely to have that
same problem later.

Can I Fix This?

I don't want you to default to self-reliance or go into fix-it
mode. But I do want you to honestly evaluate and come up with
possible solutions to the question, Can I fix this?

Hold up! When you read this, you might think, *This is too
much for me. No, Bianca! I can't fix* _____ *(fill in the blank).*
But before you count yourself out, call yourself up. Believe and bet
on yourself to come up with possible solutions to your frustrations.

Here are some examples:

I don't feel pursued. → Initiate connection and express a need
for reciprocity.

I don't feel efficient at work. → Ask to work from home one
day a week.

I don't feel appreciated. → Communicate what you need in
order to feel seen.

I don't feel important or needed. → Ask for more
responsibility.

I don't feel valued. → Request compensation or identify what

you need to feel there is a fair exchange of value you add
to work or a relationship.

I don't know how to communicate. → I'm willing to meet
with a therapist to help me develop new conflict
resolution skills.

Before we blame other people for our sadness, frustration, disappointment, or anger, what are simple ways we can take initiative? You might be the solution to your problem. Do the work to fight for solutions because no matter where you go, there will always be problems. Learn to be a problem solver for your own life.

Is It Me?

Gird your loins, friend. This is a tough question to answer, and the only one who can truly answer it is you: Are you the reason you're unhappy in life?

There are lots of legitimate reasons you might be frustrated with your life. Maybe you're dealing with a family issue that's far from being resolved. Perhaps your relationships feel stuck and stale. Or maybe you don't see your current job as your dream job. I validate that all your issues might be true. But what is your role in personal happiness and satisfaction?

If you switch friend groups every year . . .
If you have a history of working a job for six to eight months
before leaving . . .
If you can't settle down in a romantic relationship . . .
If you can't stick to a healthy lifestyle . . .
. . . then it's worth asking whether the issue is you.

If you're not content in this season of life, I'm not sure you'll find satisfaction in your next.

To help us evaluate what we are taking ownership in, let's look at possible choices and consequences so we don't blame others:

I never want to work weekends or overtime. → I understand I will most likely have to adhere to a tight budget.

I don't want to deprive myself of desserts. → I understand I can't be upset with my weight or pant size.

I don't want to ever have a boss. → I understand I'm solely responsible for my finances or lack thereof.

I don't want to change. → I understand this might compromise new relationships from forming or current relationships from growing.

The question "Is it me?" allows us to evaluate what part we play in our own contentment. It also forces us to identify what we need or will not compromise on. But when we identify our role in our own happiness and desires, we are empowered to either accept or rethink our decisions.

Is This the Best Decision for My Future?

If you're considering quitting a job, a position, a friendship, or a career, make sure you aren't running *from* something but running *to* something. Before you throw in the towel, I want you to do the following three things:

1. Talk to three wise people in various stages of life.

    Don't just ask your disgruntled peers or coworkers about a big decision. Speak to three people who don't have anything to gain or lose from your decision. Get their perspectives.

2. Pray. And I mean pray *seriously*.

   Maybe you've never prayed before. No problem! Now is a great time to start. Prayer is simply a conversation with God where you get to pour out your concerns and believe that He will speak to you in His time.

3. Consider the cost.

   If you walk away, what are you going to lose? Will quitting make you better or worse off? Are you running away because you are tired or are you stepping into something better that will aid you in your purpose in life?

And for the love of Philemon, if you do decide to move on, leave well. Here are a few tips I want you to adhere to after you have discussed this decision with wise people, prayed about it, and considered the cost:

- Leave your job, your position, your relationship better than you found it.

  If you can leave a role having made a positive impact for good, everyone wins.
- Your last impression is lasting.

  You have a choice to leave a *hero* or a *zero*, so leave well.
- What's said in private always becomes public.

  Watch your words because what is said in the dark always comes to light.
- You can never go wrong doing right.

  No matter how people treat you, honor those above you, honor those below you, honor those around you.

- Be proud of how you ended.

    Love well even if it hurts.

If this decision is best for your future, then throw in the towel and walk away with your head held high.

Am I Released?

The first time I heard this question, I was in a very dark place. My life felt unsettled, everything was in flux, and I felt like I was juggling balls and spinning plates. In a moment of vulnerability, I shared with a coworker the pain I was experiencing and frustration I felt at work. With a serious look and honest tone she asked, "Are you released?"

I stared at her, confused. "What does that even mean?" She explained that, as believers who are empowered to hear the voice of God, we will know and sense and feel when our season is done. There are *commitments*, and there are *covenants*. Covenants are designed for a lifetime and include things like marriage, spiritual agreements (like Jonathan promising to serve King David heart and soul in 1 Samuel 20:17), and other binding agreements. But commitments have an end point—when the role is filled, the job complete, or the task is done.

I made a commitment in my job to fulfill my role and make the organization better. *How is that evaluated?* We have to chat with God and ask Him, "Am I released?" In our pain, in our sadness, and in our despair, we might want to decide our jobs are done or our roles completed. But if the Lord doesn't release us, we have to believe there is still more work to be done—and to be done well.

This question is the hardest to wrestle with and the hardest to receive an answer. The word *released* isn't something you will see theologically explained or labeled explicitly in Scripture. However, we see where it is definitely implied, specifically in the life of Paul the Apostle in Acts 16. Paul was on a journey to preach the gospel and wanted to go into the province of Asia. But repeatedly the Holy Spirit didn't release Paul and his companions into that region:

> Paul and his companions traveled throughout the region of Phrygia and Galatia, having been kept by the Holy Spirit from preaching the word in the province of Asia. When they came to the border of Mysia, they tried to enter Bithynia, but the Spirit of Jesus would not allow them to. (Acts 16:6–7)

For some reason, Paul and his friends weren't allowed to go to Asia. And for some reason, I wasn't allowed to quit my job. I knew I wasn't released from my role; there was more work to be done. If you are not released from your season, don't quit. Don't step out of the place and position God has put you in because there is something specific He wants to teach you.

You might feel like a boxer backed into the corner, deciding whether to back down or fight. You might be tired. You might feel beat up. But there's still fight in you! Don't throw in the towel before it's time. Yes, life is tough—but so are you. And there's a good chance you'll discover the fighter in you is stronger than you think.

Thankfulness, Gratitude, and Contentment

I am not saying this because I am in need, for I have learned to be content whatever the circumstances. I know what it is to be in need, and I know what it is to have plenty. I have learned the secret of being content in any and every situation, whether well fed or hungry, whether living in plenty or in want.

PAUL THE APOSTLE (PHILIPPIANS 4:11–12)

What is the one thing we think we will never have? Enough. Let's get real: we live in a *more more-more* culture. We want it; we get it. We see it; we buy it. More is more.

In the beginning of creation, Adam and Eve were given access to everything in the garden, except for one single tree. They literally had everything they needed, but it wasn't enough. They wanted that *one* thing they couldn't have.

In the Genesis 3 narrative, we read about a cunning serpent who used the power of temptation to lure Eve. Temptation worked then, and it works now. God gives us plenty, yet we are tempted to believe that if we just had that *one* thing, we'd feel better, live better, and be better. But the idea of *more* is as deceptive as the serpent in the garden of Eden. As in, we want *more* because *more* is better, and we will feel better.

Maybe you are thinking, *But, Bianca, what I want isn't dangerous or evil. I mean, my list isn't that big. And if it doesn't really hurt me, why does it matter if I just want a few things? Really, what could happen?* The good news is the Bible answers that question.

There's an account in the book of Numbers where God gives His people everything they asked for. What do you think happened to them? Let's find out.

The story is told in Numbers 11, and the abbreviated version goes a little something like this: The people of God were enslaved in Egypt. They told God, "If You would just deliver us out of slavery by the Egyptians, we would be grateful, we would praise Your name, and we would never want anything ever again!"

So God, in His kindness and mercy, delivered them out of slavery.

But the children of Israel wanted more. "You know what else, God? We want some wealth. We've been slaves so long, we have no money. Just pour out some riches on us, and we won't have to ask You for anything else."

God enabled the Israelites to plunder Egypt. They were freed from slavery, *and* they were wealthy.

But was that enough? Nope.

Next, they asked for protection. And in God's merciful kindness, He gave them a cloud to cover them by day and a fire to guide them by night. And because God is loving and good, He also gave them a promise for a land for them to inherit.

But it still wasn't enough.

God was leading the people in the desert to the promised land, and now they said, "God, we need water." So God provided water.

Then they said, "God, we need food." And God gave them manna, which is a substance they could grind up and make into a powder and cook. The children of Israel had boiled manna, baked manna, fried manna, dried manna, manna sandwiches, and manna-cotti, and the ones with the real flavor made *mann*uedo.

Now they had everything they wanted, right? Wrong.

They got tired of manna and complained, "God, while we were slaves in Egypt, we had leeks, garlic, and onions. Now all we have is manna. We want meat."

When you read the narrative, it sounds as if they just need one more thing. If they have this *one* more thing, they will be content. So God basically said, "I'm going to give you meat. But it's not just going to be for a day or a week. I'm going to give you meat for a whole month" (Numbers 11:18–20). God sent them quail and the people ended up gorging themselves, many to the point of *actual* death. Numbers 11:34 documents that this location is called Kibroth Hattaavah ("the graves of greediness")[2] because they buried the people who had craved to the point of death.

The desire for *more* literally killed them.

I love the way Psalm 106 describes this very incident. "He [God] gave them exactly what they asked for—but along with it they got an empty heart" (v. 15 MSG). So there's the answer to the question: *What would happen to you if you got everything that you wanted in life?* You would have an empty heart, and you would die in a grave of greediness.

Sounds harsh? I get it. But we need to understand temptation and acknowledge that what we desire will never be enough to satisfy our earthly needs.

Do you know the most repeated phrase in Scripture? Before you guess "Fear not," let me spare you. That's the number one *command*. But the number one phrase in all of Scripture is, "Give thanks to the LORD, for he is good! His faithful love endures forever" (for example, Psalm 107:1; 118:1; 136:1 NLT).

Why do you suppose that is? I'd offer it's the phrase we need to recite most often. It's the phrase that we need to burn deep in our hearts. It's the phrase we should memorize and say repeatedly: "Give thanks to the Lord, for He is good. His love endures forever."

You might be sitting here thinking, *Wait. I'm a grateful person.*

My heart bursts with thanksgiving. Skkkkrt, hold up. Statistically speaking, we grossly misgauge our gratitude. In short, we think we are more grateful than we actually are.

Harvard University designed an actual rubric to gauge gratitude, but first I'm going to show you what God's Word says it takes to be grateful. It's more than some rote behavior change. True gratitude is transformational. Psalm 100:4 makes it so simple: "Enter [God's presence] with the password: 'Thank you!'" (MSG).

Thankfulness

Everything of value these days, everything important that we need to get into, seems to have a password. Our Wi-Fi. Our cell phones. Our bank accounts. Passwords are the key to accessing what we need most. And infinitely more than we need a news update, a phone call, or a little spending cash, we *need* to enter the presence of God. The psalmist gave us the singular password to get there: *thank You.*

This is what we need to practice.

When you wake up in the morning with the ability to open your eyes and breathe—*thank You.*
When you take a sip of a warm coffee or bite into a piece of toast—*thank You.*
When you step into your shower and bask under hot running water—*thank You.*
When you relish the beauty of the sunrise—*thank You.*

Thankful people say thank you. Don't miss a single opportunity.

I believe the leading indicator for a healthy spiritual life is growth in thankfulness and gratitude. But lots of things can stand in the way of our gratitude. One major hurdle is grumbling.

Let's take a little inventory: Have you complained about something in the past week? The traffic? Your workload? Your spouse? Your lack of spouse? Try to catch yourself every time you complain this week. It's astounding how often we do it without even thinking. Next week, cut that number at least in half.

Complaining literally destroys us. Take a look at the children of Israel, who were freed from slavery and died in the wilderness, consumed by their own constant complaining. I don't want that for you. I don't want that for me. I want us to remember to "Give thanks to the LORD, for he is good. His love endures forever."

Gratitude

I love when science and research back up what the Bible has always said. Some researchers got together and decided to uncover all the truths they could about thankfulness. Their first step was to define a thankful person. I'm going to give you *their* researched definition. This is science! Try measuring your thankfulness using these parameters instead of your own.

Is there a difference between being thankful and being grateful? Yes. "Thankfulness is an emotion, gratitude is an attitude of appreciation under any circumstance. Gratitude involves being thankful, but it is more than that. Gratitude means expressing thankfulness and being appreciative of life daily even when nothing exciting happens."[3]

Once the research was compiled, they discovered that a grateful person might do these two things on a daily basis. You ready?

1. They write a list of five things for which they are grateful.
2. They share some or all of that list twice a day with two different people.[4]

According to research coming out of the University of California, Berkeley, gratitude reprograms our brains. Researchers discovered that when you practice gratitude, you're more creative, you're more energetic, you're more optimistic, you're more socially connected, you're healthier, you're more forgiving, you're more generous, you're more joyful, and you're better looking (the last one I just made up, but people who possess all these qualities are generally pretty attractive, aren't they?).[5]

The Bible says when you're grateful, you have entered the presence of God, and it transforms you.

Sidenote for the men who will read this book: studies have shown the magnitude of gratitude, and they also found out that gratitude is harder for men to express than it is for women. Listen, brothers, it's harder for you to be grateful, and the reason (according to research)[6] is that when men say thank you, it causes them to feel indebted, obligated, and anxious. In short, it takes more courage for them to say thank you.

But here's the good news: men get an even greater return. Guys, when you say thank you, just in life on a regular basis—or better yet, on a list that you share with others—it transforms your brain at a higher rate than that of women. Gratitude is transformative! You want to be grateful.

Over time I've learned one definition of gratitude that I love. It's worth writing on a Post-it Note or jotting somewhere in your journal: *gratitude is wanting what I have.*

Grateful people want what they have.

Contentment

A pastor friend of mine conducted an informal research study attempting to disprove that if people had just 10 percent more, they would be content. So he gathered various groups of people in various income brackets. Do you know what his case study proved? People who had 10 percent more than those in the lower bracket believed that if *they* had 10 percent more money, they would be content. And the people in the highest bracket thought that if they had 10 percent more money, *they* would be content. But if what you have doesn't determine whether you're satisfied, true contentment isn't derived from anywhere outside you. It has to come from within.

This truth is crucial to our joy. In Philippians 4, we are told that Paul learned to be content in all seasons—well-fed or hungry, living in plenty or in want. We can absolutely learn this too. We can level up our gratitude practice and transform our hearts and minds as we enter the presence of the Lord with thanksgiving. And why wouldn't we give thanks to the Lord? "He is good. His love endures forever."

15 REMINDERS FROM PAUL THE APOSTLE

Do not conform to the pattern of this world, but be transformed by the renewing of your mind.

ROMANS 12:2

We are afflicted in every way, but not crushed; perplexed, but not driven to despair; persecuted, but not forsaken; struck down, but not destroyed.

2 CORINTHIANS 4:8–9 ESV

I can do everything through Christ, who gives me strength.

PHILIPPIANS 4:13 NLT

For when I am weak, then I am strong.

2 CORINTHIANS 12:10

If God is for us, who can be against us?

ROMANS 8:31

Do not be anxious about anything, but in every situation, by prayer and petition, with thanksgiving, present your requests to God.

PHILIPPIANS 4:6

We walk by faith, not by sight.

2 CORINTHIANS 5:7 ESV

Therefore, if anyone is in Christ, he is a new creation. The old has passed away; behold, the new has come.

2 CORINTHIANS 5:17 ESV

Owe nothing to anyone—except for your obligation to love one another.

ROMANS 13:8 NLT

Let us not become weary in doing good, for at the proper time we will reap a harvest if we do not give up.

GALATIANS 6:9

Not that I have already attained, or am already perfected; but I press on, that I may lay hold of that for which Christ Jesus has also laid hold of me.

PHILIPPIANS 3:12 NKJV

Hope does not disappoint.

ROMANS 5:5 NKJV

In everything give thanks.

1 THESSALONIANS 5:18 NKJV

And my God will meet all your needs according to the riches of his glory in Christ Jesus.

PHILIPPIANS 4:19

Finally, brothers and sisters, whatever is true, whatever is noble, whatever is right, whatever is pure, whatever is lovely, whatever is admirable—if anything is excellent or praiseworthy—think about such things. Whatever you have learned or received or heard from me, or seen in me—put it into practice. And the God of peace will be with you.

PHILIPPIANS 4:8–9

ACKNOWLEDGMENTS

In the act of practicing thankfulness (as I wrote in the appendix), I want to list ten things I'm grateful for and share them here:

1. I'm thankful for *you* and your willingness to buy this book. If you were in front of me, I'd pull you in for a big hug and tell you I'm proud of you. *We* aren't giving up, and *we* are in this together. This is hard work, but I know deep in my bones the hard work of obedience will pay off.

2. I'm thankful for the group of readers who willingly read this manuscript—out of order and in embryotic form—and gave their insights and honest truths. Your time was a gift to me, and I can't thank you enough.

3. I'm thankful for the amazing team at W Publishing— specifically Stephanie Newton and Lauren Bridges—for their patience with me on citing sources, footnotes, cover design, and deadlines. You have made my experience a joy, and I'm so grateful for our time around my dining room table dreaming what this book could be.

4. I'm thankful to the In The Name of Love team (Mari, Meg, Hannah, Vannessa, and Kayleigh) for being a joy to love and lead. Whether it's editing a podcast or designing

a PDF, your work is reaching people across the world. I'm honored to serve you and grateful to know you. Thank you for your yes.

5. I'm thankful for the staff and people of The Father's House Orange County, who give me grace, motivate me to keep leading, and see a vision that is only possible with God. I'm honored to lead you and love you like my family. Thank you for trusting me.

6. I'm thankful for the friends who have been by my side as confidants and defenders in such a crazy season. From traveling the globe to dining around tables, I'm forever grateful to confide, celebrate, and cheers to all that God has done in our lives. Global Gangsters, ride or die.

7. I'm thankful for my crazy family (Papi, Murmykins, Jahbee, Chu, Lunita, Alec Walec, Mart, Sagey, Sebby, ZoBoHo, and Ivey) for their continuous love and support. Until the day I die, I will feed you at my table as a way to show how much I love you. Thank you for giving me grace to be me.

8. I'm thankful for Melanie Nyema, who fought for me to make this book better, edited with all capital letters when she was yelling at me, and refused to give up on me or this project. You have been the single most important person to help me see my value as a writer, and I hope we can do this forever.

9. I'm thankful for Matthew (a.k.a. *mi amor*) (a.k.a. cuddlebug) (a.k.a. Harry) (a.k.a. Big Angel) for creating space and time for me to birth this book into the world. Without him, I would be half the woman I am today. I smother that man with hugs and kisses because it's the only way to convey how much I truly love him. Till death do us part!

10. I'm thankful for Paul the Apostle and his unwavering commitment to Christ. When people abandoned him, betrayed him, and insulted him, he remained faithful to the call on his life. I want to do the same.

NOTES

Introduction

1. Kelly Jensen, "Over 50% of Adults Have Not Finished a Book in the Last Year," Book Riot, June 21, 2022, http://bookriot.com /american-reading-habits-2022.

Chapter 1

1. Carol S. Dweck, *Mindset: The New Psychology of Success* (New York: Random House, 2006), 7.
2. Dweck, *Mindset*, 6.
3. Dweck, 7.
4. Dweck, 5, 7.

Chapter 2

1. *Merriam-Webster*, s.v. "perseverance (*n.*)," accessed February 22, 2023, https://www.merriam-webster.com/dictionary/perseverance.
2. Angela Lee Duckworth, "Grit: The Power of Passion and Perseverance," TED Talk, May 9, 2013, www.ted.com/talks/angela _lee_duckworth_grit_the_power_of_passion_and_perseverance /transcript.
3. Duckworth, "Grit: The Power of Passion and Perseverance."
4. Alexander MacLaren, "Why Saul Became Paul," Blue Letter Bible, accessed February 20, 2023, https://www.blueletterbible.org/comm

/maclaren_alexander/expositions-of-holy-scripture/acts/why-saul
-became-paul.cfm.

Chapter 3

1. Diane Coutu, "How Resilience Works," *Harvard Business Review*
   (Boston: Harvard Business Review Press, 2002), 10, https://hbr.org
   /2002/05/how-resilience-works.
2. Eric Greitens, *Resilience: Hard-Won Wisdom for Living a Better Life*
   (New York: Houghton Mifflin Harcourt, 2015), 30.
3. Coutu, "How Resilience Works."
4. Coutu, "How Resilience Works."

Chapter 4

1. Eugene Peterson, *A Long Obedience in the Same Direction* (Downers
   Grove, IL: InterVarsity, 2021), 5.
2. Don Schlitz, "The Gambler," *The Gambler*, Sony/ATV Music
   Publishing, 1978, https://www.songfacts.com/lyrics/kenny-rogers
   /the-gambler.
3. *Merriam-Webster*, s.v. "infidelity (*n.*)," accessed February 23, 2023,
   https://www.merriam-webster.com/dictionary/infidelity.
4. John Mark Comer, *The Ruthless Elimination of Hurry: How to Stay
   Emotionally Healthy and Spiritually Alive in the Chaos of the Modern
   World* (Colorado Springs: WaterBrook, 2019); Peter Scazzero,
   *Emotionally Healthy Spirituality: It's Impossible to Be Spiritually
   Mature While Remaining Emotionally Immature* (Grand Rapids:
   Zondervan, 2017); Wayne Cordeiro, *Leading on Empty: Refilling
   Your Tank and Renewing Your Passion* (Bloomington, MN: Bethany
   House, 2009).

Chapter 6

1. David L. Thompson with Gina Thompson Eickhoff, *God's Healing
   for Hurting Families: Biblical Principles for Reconciliation and
   Recovery* (Indianapolis: Wesleyan Publishing House, 2004), 7.
2. "Anistemi," New Testament Greek Lexicon, Bible Study Tools,

accessed January 24, 2023, https://www.biblestudytools.com
/lexicons/greek/nas/anistemi.html.

Chapter 7

1. Substance Abuse and Mental Health Services Administration,
   "Understanding the Impact of Trauma," in *Trauma-Informed Care
   in Behavioral Health Services*, Treatment Improvement Protocol
   (TIP) Series, no. 57, HHS Publication No. (SMA) 13–4801
   (Rockville, MD: Center for Substance Abuse Treatment, 2014),
   https://www.ncbi.nlm.nih.gov/books/NBK207191/.
2. Federico Bermúdez-Rattoni, ed., *Neural Plasticity and Memory:
   From Genes to Brain Imaging*, Frontiers in Neuroscience (Boca
   Raton, FL: CRC Press/Taylor & Francis, 2007), https://www.ncbi
   .nlm.nih.gov/books/NBK1850/.
3. "Prefrontal Cortex," The Science of Psychotherapy, January 4, 2017,
   https://www.thescienceofpsychotherapy.com/prefrontal-cortex/.
4. Rick Hanson, *Hardwiring Happiness: The New Brain Science
   of Contentment, Calm, and Confidence* (New York: Harmony
   Publishing, 2013), 23.
5. Hanson, *Hardwiring Happiness*, 42.
6. Kristin Neff, "Definition of Self-Compassion," Self-Compassion.
   org, accessed February 24, 2023, https://self-compassion.org/the
   -three-elements-of-self-compassion-2/.
7. Debbie Hampton, "Everything Your Brain Needs to Know About
   Mindfulness," The Best Brain Possible, December 20, 2020,
   https://thebestbrainpossible.com/mindfulness-brain-mental-health
   /#:~:text=Over%20time%2C%20consistently%20practicing%20
   mindful,control%20more%20of%20the%20time.
8. Check out the appendix for fifteen of my favorite Paul verses I turn
   to for encouragement.
9. "Why Is the News Always So Depressing?" The Decision Lab,
   accessed February 24, 2023, https://thedecisionlab.com/biases
   /negativity-bias.
10. Jon Gordon, "The Surprising Power of Thank You," *Full Focus*,

accessed February 27, 2023, https://fullfocus.co/gratitude-and
-happiness.

11. Robert A. Emmons and Michael E. McCullough, "Counting
Blessings versus Burdens: An Experimental Investigation of
Gratitude and Subjective Well-Being in Daily Life," *Journal of
Personality and Social Psychology* 84, no. 2 (2003): 377–89, https://
doi.org/10.1037/0022-3514.84.2.377.

12. Marla Tabaka, "Giving Thanks Can Make You Happier,
According to Years of Research," *Inc.*, November 25, 2019, https://
www.inc.com/marla-tabaka/giving-thanks-can-make-you-happier
-according-to-years-of-research.html.

Chapter 8

1. "Bringing Up Two at Once," *New York Times*, May 24, 1964,
https://www.nytimes.com/1964/05/24/archives/bringing-up-two
-at-once.html.

Chapter 10

1. "Working Out Boosts Brain Health," American Psychological
Association, March 4, 2020, https://www.apa.org/topics/exercise
-fitness/stress.

2. Julia C. Basso and Wendy A. Suzuki, "The Effects of Acute Exercise
on Mood, Cognition, Neurophysiology, and Neurochemical
Pathways: A Review," *Brain Plasticity* 2, no. 2 (March 28, 2017):
127–52, https://doi.org/10.3233/BPL-160040.

3. Wendy Suzuki, "A Neuroscientist Shares the 4 Brain-Changing
Benefits of Exercise—and How Much She Does Every Week,"
CNBC, October 22, 2021, https://www.cnbc.com/2021/10/22
/neuroscientist-shares-the-brain-health-benefits-of-exercise-and
-how-much-she-does-a-week.html.

4. Kirsten Weir, "Nurtured by Nature," *Monitor on Psychology* 51,
no. 3 (April 2020), https://www.apa.org/monitor/2020/04/nurtured
-nature.

5. Bill Frist, "The Science Behind How Nature Affects Your

Health," *Forbes*, June 15, 2017, https://www.forbes.com/sites/bill frist/2017/06/15/the-science-behind-how-nature-affects-your-health /?sh=754d96a015ae.

6. Weir, "Nurtured by Nature."

7. Darby E. Saxbe and Rena Repetti, "No Place Like Home: Home Tours Correlate with Daily Patterns of Mood and Cortisol," *Personality and Social Psychology Bulletin* 36, no. 1 (2010): 71–81, https://doi.org/10.1177/0146167209352864.

8. Martin Lang et al., "Effects of Anxiety on Spontaneous Ritualized Behavior," *Current Biology* 25, no. 14 (June 18, 2015): 1892–7, https://doi.org/10.1016/j.cub.2015.05.049.

9. Adam W. Hanley et al., "Washing Dishes to Wash the Dishes: Brief Instruction in an Informal Mindfulness Practice," *Mindfulness* 6 (2015): 1095–1103, https://doi.org/10.1007/s12671 -014-0360-9.

10. "A Clean, Well-Lighted Place: How Less Clutter Can Reduce Stress," BeWell, Stanford University, accessed February 25, 2023, https://bewell.stanford.edu/a-clean-well-lighted-place/.

11. Tasha Cobbs Leonard feat. Kierra Sheard, "Put a Praise on It," *One Place Live* (Santa Monica, CA: Motown Gospel, 2015).

12. As Paul said in 2 Corinthians 3:17, "Where the Spirit of the Lord is, there is freedom."

13. Jen Rose Smith, "Anxiety Might Make You a Bad Decision Maker," KOMU, updated October 30, 2020, https://www.komu.com/news /anxiety-might-make-you-a-bad-decision-maker/article_a5c6f4d4 -ffa7-5538-832c-7cbf0ff6ccd1.html.

14. Julie Marks, "Grounding Exercises: Using Your 5 Senses for Anxiety Relief," Psych Central, October 8, 2021, https://psych central.com/anxiety/using-the-five-senses-for-anxiety-relief#using -your-senses.

Chapter 11

1. While frequently attributed to Lao Tzu, among others, this quote likely "evolved over a long period of time" but in its current form

can be attributed to Frank Outlaw. See "Watch Your Thoughts, They Become Words; Watch Your Words, They Become Actions," Quote Investigator, January 10, 2013, https://quoteinvestigator.com /2013/01/10/watch-your-thoughts/.

Chapter 12

1. A. T. Robertson, "Word Pictures in the New Testament," StudyLight.org, accessed February 26, 2023, https://www.study light.org/commentaries/eng/rwp/philippians-2.html.
2. Nate Saint, as quoted in "Why You Should 'Waste Your Life'— Nate Saint," Deeper Christian Quotes, August 13, 2020, https:// deeperchristianquotes.com/why-you-should-waste-your-life-nate -saint/.

Chapter 13

1. Strong's Greek Lexicon, s.v. "hypernikaō (v.)," Blue Letter Bible, accessed February 26, 2023, https://www.blueletterbible.org /lexicon/g5245/kjv/tr/0–1/.

Appendix

1. The Free Dictionary, "throw in the sponge/towel," accessed February 26, 2023, http://idioms.thefreedictionary.com/throw+in +the+sponge%2Ftowel.
2. John W. Ritenbaugh, "What the Bible Says About Kibroth Hattaavah," Bible Tools, accessed February 26, 2023, https://www .bibletools.org/index.cfm/fuseaction/Topical.show/RTD/cgg/ID /2932/Kibroth-Hattaavah.htm.
3. Psychiatric Medical Care Communications Team, "The Difference Between Gratitude and Thankfulness," Psychiatric Medical Care, accessed February 26, 2023, https://www.psychmc.com/blogs /difference-between-gratitude-and-thankfulness.
4. Michael Craig Miller, "In Praise of Gratitude," Harvard Health Publishing, November 21, 2012, https://www.health.harvard.edu /blog/in-praise-of-gratitude-201211215561.

5. Summer Allen, "The Science of Gratitude," Greater Good Science Center at UC Berkeley, May 2018, https://ggsc.berkeley.edu/images/uploads/GGSC-JTF_White_Paper-Gratitude-FINAL.pdf.
6. Allen, "The Science of Gratitude."

ABOUT THE
AUTHOR

Bianca Juárez Olthoff is president of In The Name of Love ministry, host of the *We're Going There* podcast, and author of the bestselling books *Play with Fire* and *How to Have Your Life Not Suck*. But to her friends and family, she is a girl who loves to serve up hot meals around her dinner table, create places for those who don't fit in, and preach freedom for those who can't find a way out.

Bianca lives in Orange County, California, with her family and loves leading alongside her husband, Matt, as proud pastors of The Father's House OC. You can connect with her on social media or invite her for a speaking event by visiting www.BiancaOlthoff.com.

From the Publisher

GREAT BOOKS

ARE EVEN BETTER WHEN THEY'RE SHARED!

Help other readers find this one:

- Post a review at your favorite online bookseller

- Post a picture on a social media account and share why you enjoyed it

- Send a note to a friend who would also love it—or better yet, give them a copy

Thanks for reading!